ONLY FRAGMENTS FOUND

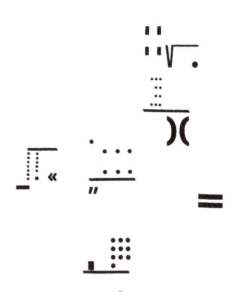

giovanna sandri

only fragments found

selected poems
1969-1998

Edited by Guy Bennett

*Translated from the Italian
by Guy Bennett, Faust Pauluzzi,
& Giovanna Sandri*

*And with an Introduction
by Giulia Niccolai*

OTIS BOOKS | SEISMICITY EDITIONS
The Graduate Writing program
Otis College of Art and Design
LOS ANGELES · 2014

Book design and typesetting: Guy Bennett

ISBN-10: 0-9860173-1-0
ISBN-13: 978-0-9860173-1-5

OTIS BOOKS | SEISMICITY EDITIONS
The Graduate Writing program
Otis College of Art and Design
9045 Lincoln Boulevard
Los Angeles, CA 90045

www.otis.edu/graduate-writing/seismicity-editions
seismicity@otis.edu

Contents

Note on the Present Edition

The publication of this book is the realization of a dream deferred. Ever since I first encountered the poetry of Giovanna Sandri in early 1995, I have wished that a broad selection of her writing were available for anglophone readers. At last it is.

Not that her work was wholly unknown in English: two of her books (*da K a S: dimora dell'asimmetrico* | *from K to S: dwelling of the asymmetric* and *le dieci porte di Zhuang-zi* | *the ten Gates of Zhuang-zi*) were originally published in bilingual editions and a third (*clessidra: il ritmo delle tracce*) later translated into English; a dozen or so of her poems were also included in two American anthologies (*Italian Poetry, 1960–1980: from Neo to Post Avant-Garde* and *The Promised Land: Italian Poetry After 1975*), and individual translations occasionally appeared in journals. That said, many works remained untranslated, and virtually all of her publications are long out of print and often difficult to find. For these reasons, as well as for the pleasure of being able to share her work with new readers, I am especially pleased that the present edition is now available. Given the somewhat unorthodox presentation of its contents, I would like to say a few words about it.

only fragments found includes a range of texts – whether complete works, excerpts, or individual poems, some previously published, some not – from over the course of Giovanna Sandri's career. Some of these works are purely visual, others purely verbal, and still others a mix of the two. Furthermore, knowing English, Sandri not only translated some of her own work into that language, she also occasionally wove English lines into otherwise Italian poems, and thus a few texts are either entirely bilingual or include passages in both languages.

This variety posed an interesting problem for the composition of this volume: some books (*da K a S...*, *le dieci porte...*) would have to be run bilingually, since they were conceived of and designed as such, the original editions presenting the dual-language text on facing pages. Other books (*dal canguro all'aithyia (o come farsi scrittura), clessidra...*) could not be presented this way, since they combine verbal and visual texts on facing pages, leaving no possibility for an *en face* presentation of the translation.

After some head-scratching, I opted for what appeared a rational if unorthodox solution to this dilemma: a bilingual, *en face* presentation for those works that either needed or could accomodate one, and a sequential presentation, with the English translation appearing after the Italian original, for those that could not. In this way, each work is available in both languages in the format most appropriate to it.

I have also respected Sandri's use of pagination, which was irregular but not inconsistent: she paginated collections of individual poems (*da K a S..., clessidra...*), but not longer, single-text works (*Capitolo Zero, alfabeto / albero del Tempo, dal canguro all'aithyia..., le dieci porte...*). She may have felt that the use of page numbers emphasized the incremental, poem-by-poem progression through a book, whereas their absence suggested an uninterrupted textual flow. Whatever the case may be, I have followed her lead, and for this reason some works are paginated, others not.

Finally, I have retained the use of a monowidth typeface in *da K a S...* in order to respect the modular, symmetrical design of those poems. The proportional typeface used elsewhere in the book would not have allowed the same degree of regularity in the mirroring of texts on facing pages. I trust that intentional inconsistencies such as this, as well as those noted above, will not unduly distract the reader nor detract from the poetry.

−Guy Bennett
October 2013

Introduction

As I glanced through the PDF of the first concrete poems in Giovanna Sandri's book, *Chapter Zero* of 1969, sent by Guy Bennett, to my great surprise I discovered a joy and a grand sense of wonder immediately causing me to say: just look at the irony, the intelligence, the interior space we possessed in those years!

I don't know why – perhaps because I hadn't seen Giovanna's work in quite some time – she, more than anyone else in all these years, brought to mind the spirit of that time, the lightness, the happiness. Not only to her, but to *all of us* during that period, I attribute the gifts, the talents I've just named.

Giovanna clearly succeeded in realizing this on each page, thanks to a simple use of Letraset (commas, periods, parentheses, etc.), though elaborated with the rigor, the patience and the devotion of a "cloistered nun." A nun devoted to creating the world's most refined, "starched and pressed" embroidery.

So had Emilio Villa defined her work.

And what to say about certain pages, expanded to the point of seeming the starry heavens in a planetarium?

Or of linear poems, that Giovanna could then only compose on a typewriter? Each of them written and brought to the page so as to geometricize spaces, signaling their boundaries, like a mandala.

Take the text, "in the thirteenth book of the Light of Tantra" [pp. 78/79],* where the written words graphically create a rectangular frame around an empty, white circle. It's also worth noting that Giovanna recalls these words of Abhinavagupta, "When the magnetic field the gravitational field and the creative field coincide then there is also coincidence between stasis and movement between being and becoming." She must have chosen this particular sentence

---

* The page numbers refer to both the Italian and English texts.

out of attraction to "the creative field," but in doing so she also preferred a most valid and surprising concept, perceiving its true meaning. (Further on I will describe an event that occurred between us having this very same dynamic.)

The linear poems written in this way represent a Carthusian and unshakeable commitment, in itself a guarantee that each written term will bear a "superhuman power, in which the word is listened to in its making." Such is the interpretation of critic Graziella Pulce, who in 2003 edited *Costruire ricordi* ["Constructing Memories"] for the publisher Archinto, a book containing the correspondence between Giorgio Manganelli and Giovanna Sandri, with twenty-six letters by the great writer and Giovanna's memoir (I wrote the introduction). Pulce continues: "Giovanna Sandri's writing is uncompromising, doesn't accept half-measures: the plane upon which we meet her is the *oracular,* where every sign is an omen, sending us to yet another sign, uninterruptedly."

But where have we wound up? What is left of all that? Of that joy in making, of believing unconditionally, of that irony, that absolute beauty and elegance?

In her capacity as "oracle" foretelling the future, Giovanna writes: "from an Egyptian stele / (Dynasty XVIII) // men's hearts / are weak / they have ceased / creating / memory is no longer / return / of harmony (it deceives) // we no longer praise / (nor sing) / the original / w h i c h   e n a b l e s" [pp. 108 / 146].

That letter-spaced "w h i c h   e n a b l e s" is masterful, precisely because we are no longer able to do much, having lost touch with ourselves, no longer possessing the shadow of an interior space. We are closed, in the grip of negative emotions: anger, bitterness, envy. Always chasing around for something, never satisfied.

Giovanna foresees these first ten years of the third millennium, or is it from the 18th Egyptian Dynasty that we have been conscious of the phenomenon which keeps repeating itself cyclically, every so many years?

Giovanna's culture goes back to our civilization's most remote periods, urgent to discover and understand our deepest roots.

Indeed, by analogy with "roots," Giovanna gives this title to one of her investigations into this subject: *alphabet/tree of Time,* from 1977. She posits that "Hermes / brought the arboreal alphabet / from Greece to Egypt / then back / again / from Egypt to Greece" [pp. 86/87], and she goes on to associate the alphabet with astronomy, the musical scale, weights and measures, and *olive cultivation.* Doing so, Hermes "put / a silver egg / in the womb / of the dark // (reason of the world / suspended) // wonder of the one / limits of the other." And here the association returns: wonder and limits, because instinctually, the wonderous being a higher and magical manifestation, we are urged to think that it has no limits. Instead, it's actually the contrary. The wonderous is possible only because it is created upon a strict geometrical grid.

Like the kaleidoscope?

In the pages that follow Giovanna explains the reason for the association "trees = letters," referring "even to the letters of the ancient Irish alphabet, like that used by Welsh Druids (described by Caesar) [that] bear the names of trees." With her knowledge of classical Greek (as well as other dead languages), she carefully searches for its philological roots: "alpha from alphe (honor) alphainein (to invent)"; "aleph ox of the Phoenicians"; "time leaf page / olive tree olive / letter fruit / root (rediscovered) / between the furrows / hoe and basket / the instrument // the earth opens to the story of man…"

Up above, at the tops of most pages in *alphabet/tree of Time,* a single image of "concrete" poetry, rather large letters of an alphabet unknown to us or branches and twigs that split and divide?

The term "concrete" has never seemed so appropriate to me, as if Giovanna wanted to embody this analogy "trees = letters" to feel herself always surrounded and protected by the "word," sound of spoken words (sound and air), sound that disperses in air or engraved sign, furrow: "the earth opens to the story of man." "signs climb the cliff face / (table of Time)." Memory.

Up above on the page I've cited, a kind of upside-down *y* giving the sense of being affixed to something steep, very like a wall, a movement I can't understand how Giovanna was able to create using Letraset.

So too on pp. 102 / 103, part of a *Q* that seems to fly off to the right, seen from below, by us down here on earth. A migrating bird? This the text: "the gyre of space / organized by means of lines/tensions / (zero A B) (theorem of equilibriums)…"

How is it possible not to pick up from Giovanna the sense of the sacred that language and writing held for her? An introductory universe as alchemical vehicle of research into the Self and its actual reality.

To this end I would like to note one of her statements published in the catalog for the show "Post Scriptum – Artiste in Italia tra linguaggio e immagine negli anni '60 e '70," VIII Biennale Donna, Palazzo Massari, Ferrara, aprile–giugno 1998 ["Post Scriptum–Italian Artists Between Language and Image in the Sixties and Seventies," VIII Women's Biennale, Palazzo Massari, Ferrara, April–June 1998]: "I didn't exist, there existed the external face that was articulate, that struggled… If (at school) I found principals who annoyed me I yelled, in fact I was articulate in that, though within myself I didn't exist. My work had actually become this *iter* in progress, from non-existence to being, to becoming articulate and I first passed through images that were psychologically impersonal, and then came to language… I created but I had to become articulate… I did send work to shows and I knew that I was following the right *iter*. I wasn't very interested in becoming known, a mistake perhaps, I was interested above all in working…"

For these very reasons Giovanna Sandri was recognized only within the limited circles of "insiders" of experimentalism and the avant-garde, as she was so retiring, hypersensitive and voluntarily isolated, never accepting to take part, for instance, in those literary kermesses and poetry festivals that would have made her known to a larger public.

So, I firmly believe in this book of hers published in the U.S., with the hope that from there it bounce back, returning to Europe, so that she may receive the recognition she deserves. (This type of rescue *in extremis* has already happened for other Italian authors.)

There were two poets and a very fine painter much younger than her, they too "lone wolves," who truly admired her and were her great friends: Luigi Ballerini, Nanni Cagnone and Magdalo Mussio.

An English teacher at the Liceo Giulio Cesare in Rome, for many years Giovanna took care of her ill mother who died in 1989. She never married, but she had a difficult and tempestuous relationship with Giorgio Manganelli, with whom she fortunately remained dear friends until his death in 1990 (see Managanelli's letters and Giovanna Sandri's memoir published in the aforementioned *Costruire ricordi*).

Giovanna Sandri felt herself to be "dead inside" ("I didn't exist") because of that "bewilderment still latent in me after the devastating war years (grief and massacre) that led me to shutting myself up in a defensive non-existence."

As for "the devastating war years," Giovanna meant the death at sea of her brother, a naval officer, as well as the misunderstandings and political blame assigned to her father, an Air Force general, after the liberation.

When I met Giovanna in Rome, towards the end of the sixties, I was somewhat awed by her: she was about ten years older and possessed a culture that felt much vaster and more profound than mine. (A culture that I can now define as "spiritual," a term that I had no way of recognizing then.)

We became friends in the eighties, and our friendship deepened after a conference on Manganelli held in Rome at the Teatro Argentina on December 17–18, 1997, when she published in the conference proceedings her recollection of Giorgio, *Gli anni trench* ["The Trench Coat Years"]. I'd already written about Manganelli in the article *Cavalli veri, cavalli figurati* ["Real Horses, Figurative Horses"], published in *Esoterico biliardo* ["Esoteric Billiards," Archinto, 2001]. Giovanna wanted to go ahead with her memoir of him and she sent me the various chapters one by one as she wrote them, so that we might discuss them together.

In those years, when I had to go down to Rome for work, I'd always visit her in the large apartment (it was her parents') on Via Rovereto, in the Trieste district. I had the impression that after her mother's death, she had not made the slightest change to it; she hadn't even moved a single piece of furniture in those bourgeois quarters, frozen in their respective functions, as in a thirties photo: living room, dining room, study, kitchen, etc.

Only on the walls, next to the nineteenth-century landscapes, various of her large concrete poems (very often in black and white: Letraset on cardboard), extremely modern, often with mythological titles, splendid but anachronistic and unlikely in those surroundings.

I'd always wanted to ask Giovanna if she had hung her work on the walls after her mother's death, or if she had placed them there before, but I never dared to. I had the feeling that my question would seem indiscrete and that, in some way, it might have wounded or made her suspicious, as if I were uncovering a secret. Giovanna was witty and self-ironizing but quite touchy. If she refused, impatient and cutting, any sort of impersonal conversation "in the English manner" about health and the weather, she delegated to herself the final decision about what might or might not be said. It was she who defined the limits, pretending not to have heard your question or looking at you disapprovingly.

(Now, in keeping with the fact that Giovanna hadn't moved even an ashtray in her parents' house, I'm convinced that the concrete poems were already on the study and hallway walls when her mother was still alive.)

If we would like to confirm what Giovanna wrote about herself in the catalog for the show "Post Scriptum," we should note that among the seven volumes of her concrete and linear poems comprising this American selection, the chapbook of one of her most particular moments of awareness is without a doubt *hourglass: the rhythm of traces* of 1992. On the first page of this collection, the profile of a sphinx' head made from a sheet of black paper. We interpret her angry face from the cut of the eye and eyebrow. The head itself is bristling behind with edges, and an empty, white square between the face and the mane.

The sphinx watches over the gigantic necropolis, her face muses over the one point where the sun rises. She is the guardian of the forbidden shores and the royal mummies. She listens to the song of the planets. She watches over the eternal boundary between all that has been and all that is to come. She watches the blue Nile flow far off and the sun ships sail.

If Giovanna was finally able to entrust to the sphinx the grief she'd endured, this became possible with the help of myths, something quite far off in time, but through her spirituality and sensibility very near and real for her.

Choosing honor, one chooses myth.

The *hourglass* poems have almost everything to do with time and definitely mirror her thought in respect to it.

Reading, they are perceived "wrapped in silence," as a worm is wrapped in silk.

The silence of her meditations and her days. The silence chosen and dearest to her.

These poems are longer and they tend to be laid out normally (as is *the ten Gates of Zhuang-zi*).

Various concrete poems which already appeared in her first books, are repeated identically [pp. 23 → 188, 26 → 200, 27 → 190, 39 → 206], etc., as if she no longer felt the need to create those "psychologically impersonal" images to give her strength, but was suddenly able to express her thought.

The hourglass is a spiritual archetype.

In this light, Giovanna is able to accept the thieving of time, the constant changing of things and that which it may also grant us: "the arrow / of / Time / com / pensates / what / its / trail / lets / fal / l."

The splendid poem titled "hourglass" (pp. 187/213): "a wrinkle of sand / keeps the flow / from the asphalt / of time."

Here we have a "time" dense and heavy as asphalt alongside a "wrinkle of sand," something thin and meager as the hourglass' thread.

During a retreat some fifteen years ago, I "realized," "saw," "understood for the first time" that the figure of the stylized Tibetan Buddha (thin in contrast to the Chinese Buddha), hanging on the wall in a tanka, in front of my meditation seat, was effectively composed of two triangles: the first with the vertex at the bottom and the large base at the top (the long line of the shoulders), and the one below with the vertex at the top (the two vertices meet), and the base following the line of the knees in the lotus position.

I saw this new awareness with amazement and joy, because I'd understood that the "hourglass" and its thin and meager thread of sand represent eternity that, being devoid of time, has lost its connotations of denseness and heaviness. (Unrelenting characteristics that worry and obsess many of us.)

And so I can do no less than suppose that Giovanna (choosing the "wrinkle of sand") had had a similar intuition.

Even the poem titled "reangling the axes" [pp. 191/217], "the pre / valence / of go / ing / on / rends / mourn / in / g" is proof of a most important change for which she was grateful to the flow of time.

It's no accident that the words in this text are divided up into the briefest syllables that run down the page like a very thin stream of water or sand.

I have already mentioned the fact that Giovanna was always disposed to giving natural forms to words, with the need for finding the alphabet everywhere, to feel it omnipresent (like God?).

On pp. 195/221 where the poem speaks of "sea," and in the next on pp. 197/223, in the text "on/of," where a bottle thrown into the sea "seeks / the horizon," we have many commas or very tiny squares that fall, fall down the page lending us a clear sense of depth.

But here a quotation from Plato's *Symposium,* to explain and lend new value, new sense, to her choice of verticality in certain of her poems: *"just like water flows through / a woolen thread from the fuller cup into the emptier / how fine it would be, o Glaucon, / if wisdom were made in such a way as to flow / through the letters of the alphabet / (drops the fragments)."** Water as an image of discursive flow and of the word through the "stream" of discourse.

On the other hand, in the poem "encounter" [pp. 193 / 219], these same "fragments" denote alienation, the inability to center on the author's part. So even words themselves, ordinarily faithful friends in their "expressive" capacity of helping us to understand and to live things out, become fragmented, losing their authority and force: "the crossing was / arduous and / dense with / creaking // in the words / encountered / on frag / ments found."

Although "elevated," oracular and unyielding, Giovanna's writing never shrinks from bringing to light its very *défaillances,* as its true reason for being is that of always drawing the Self closer to actual truth.

For Giovanna writing is both vehicle and result of her research.

The volume *the ten Gates of Zhuang-zi* of 1994 is written in memory of Giacinto Scelsi, musician and composer, whom she greatly admired.

She wanted to translate it herself into English. Perhaps to make this gift to her friend that much more complete: in this way even many foreign friends may read it.

The poem explores the phenomenon of sound, and unfolds as we follow a group of allegorical characters (*Intelligence, Articulation* (!), *Discursiveness,* et al) to and through the ten Gates: "passing through

---

* Actually, Sandri has "doctored" this passage from the *Symposium,* changing the identity of Socrates' (who speaks these lines) interlocutor from Agathon to Glaucon, and replacing the idea of wisdom flowing from the "fuller" to the "emptier" man with that of it flowing *"through the letters of the alphabet / (drops the fragments)."* As I was translating *clessidra,* in which this passage is quoted, I went back to the *Symposium* to verify the wording only to find that the above lines are not there. When I queried Sandri about them she replied with a laugh that she had made them up. – GB

/ the ninth Gate // (black stone / white stone) // Emblem-Bearer / came across Abandonment-of-Emblems // they exchanged / a yo-yo // resumed elliptical directions." [pp. 264/265]

Here the wonderful irony of the exchanging of yo-yos and of the elliptical directions makes us immediately visualize Giovanna's winning laughter in having created this so very happy and liberating verse.

The "Emblems." For Manganelli too "coats-of-arms" were deeply symbolic. According to Graziella Pulce, "To render the desert crossable (the condition of non-existence, the absence of words) to make of the desert a coat-of-arms is the geometricalization of spaces and the marking of a border."

Above all in the first books that comprise this selection, many brief texts, facing each other on the page, recall the powerful base of two sides of a triangle, with the vertex at the top. That of the capital A.

Even in the Sanskrit alphabet (the father of all alphabets), the A is the first letter, and as such is sacred.

We can still recall Giovanna's confession in the catalog for the show "Post Scriptum": "My work had actually become this *iter* in progress, from non-existence to being, to becoming articulate…" taken up again at the Gate *Articulation*: "slowly / (gradually) / *Articulation* approached / the first Gate // a dis / continuous staircase of letters / was Alphabet" where yet that "gradually" makes us follow her own steps toward recovery.

Two pages later, *Discursiveness*: "found halfclosed / the third Gate // too many paths / he had followed / because of / Road" with the double meaning: of *per Via*: "by way of" and "because of"….

But I've already exceeded the space allowed me. The poems in *the ten Gates of Zhuang-zi* (as I've tried to say) are the most articulated and comprehensible, and so too the "non-collected poems" such as "Arianna's Song," on pp. 302/303, in which writing is compared to weaving, to the woven fabric as an interweaving of narratives: "with / sacred skill / in tracing / you entwined / wisdom and sign / / that silent I spun into meaning."

For *the ten Gates,* Giovanna chose an Oriental culture, of which she shows, even in this case, to have known a good deal. As with the bipolar concept of Desire and Void (Vacuity).

Now, that anecdote I spoke about at the start. Four women had very different but quite important ties to Giorgio Manganelli: Ebe Flamini, Alda Merini, Giovanna Sandri and yours truly.

On the night between the 9th and 10th of December, I had a very unsettling dream about Manganelli who had left us in May. I won't tell it, as it would take up too much space, but suffice it to say that I was looking everywhere for Manganelli and I was desperate because I couldn't find him. I had even gone to Canada (ah, those three *a*'s) to search for him! In sleep, I then opened my bedroom window and found him, right there, sitting on the edge of the terrace. I heard him and understood his words even as I read them on his lips: Nilde, all is all! Nilde, all is all!

Absolutely lifelike. In his book *Il rumore sottile della prosa* ["The Subtle Sound of Prose"] he'd written: "I think of the future, my dwelling place, like a gigantic mental cube, and define it as such since I can't discern its outline. I ignore its dimensions, but I'm unable not to think that in that space there is All, but not only All as you now conceive it, but all of the Alls possible."

That morning I called Giovanna and together we took a closer look at many of the dream's details, coming to the same conclusions. Our analyses coincided.

Soon after talking with me, Giovanna received a call from Ebe Flamini, who asked for my address: she wanted to have a publisher send me a posthumous book of Giorgio's.

Giovanna, quite surprised by the coincidence, called me back to tell me about it, and in that moment Bianca Tarozzi arrived from Venice with a gift of one of Alda Merini's books. Let's have another look at Abhinavaupta's formula: "When the magnetic field the gravitational field and the creative field coincide then there is also coincidence between stasis and movement between being and becoming." That which I've just recounted, when it happened to us in the space of a few minutes (I still hear the crackling like scintillas) – with Manganelli some sort of pivot and we four drawn suddenly to the four cardinal Doors of the mandala, doesn't it seem the realization of that teaching?

None of us knew who Nilde was.

The day of Giovanna's funeral (August 2002) the priest from the church of Sant'Agnese (who conducted the funeral service and most probably had never met Giovanna, but had read her collection of poems *the ten Gates of Zhuagng-zi,* as one of her friends in attendance had given it to him), moved me by the great tribute he granted her. He confessed he felt a certain envy in respect to the writer, capable of a faith so intense and much greater than his own.

From his words, his tone of voice, his expression and gestures, I understood that he was telling the truth.

– Giulia Niccolai
July 2013

Translation: Paul Vangelisti

capitolo
zero

chapter
zero

[1969]

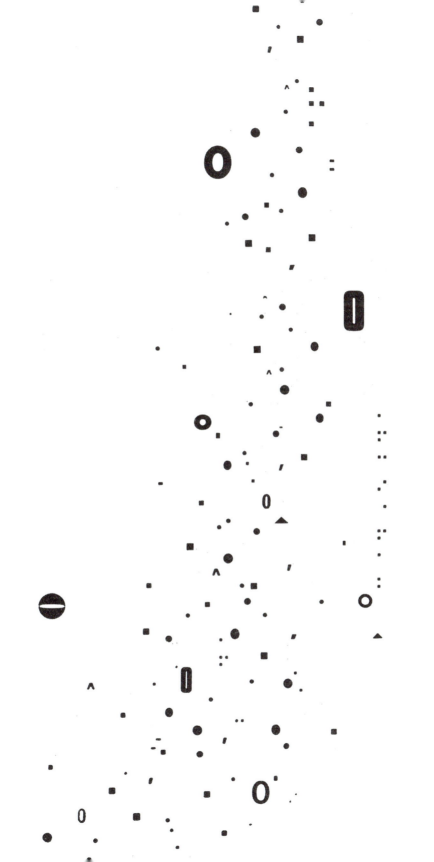

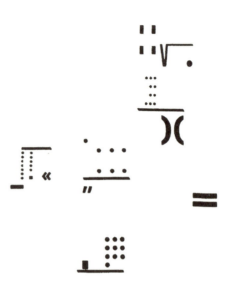

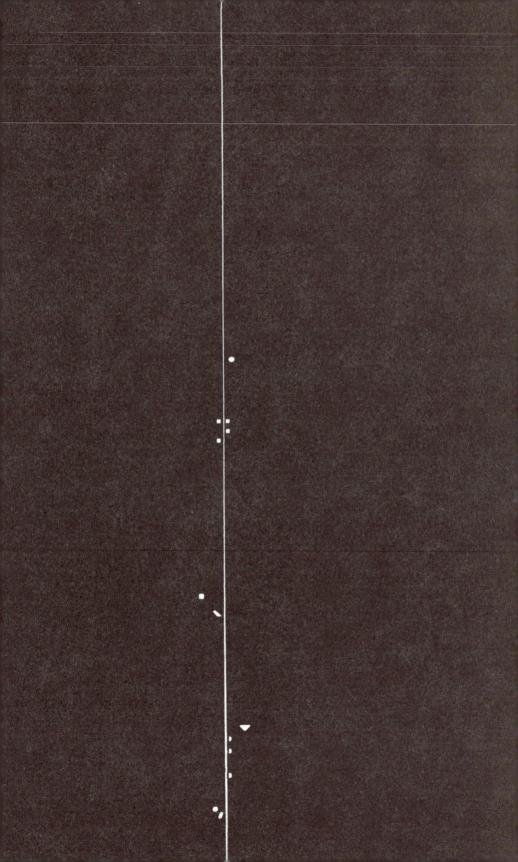

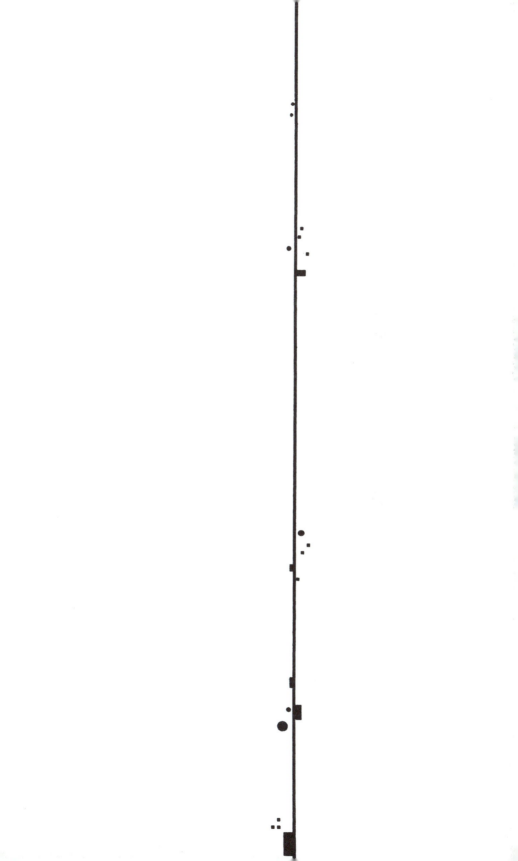

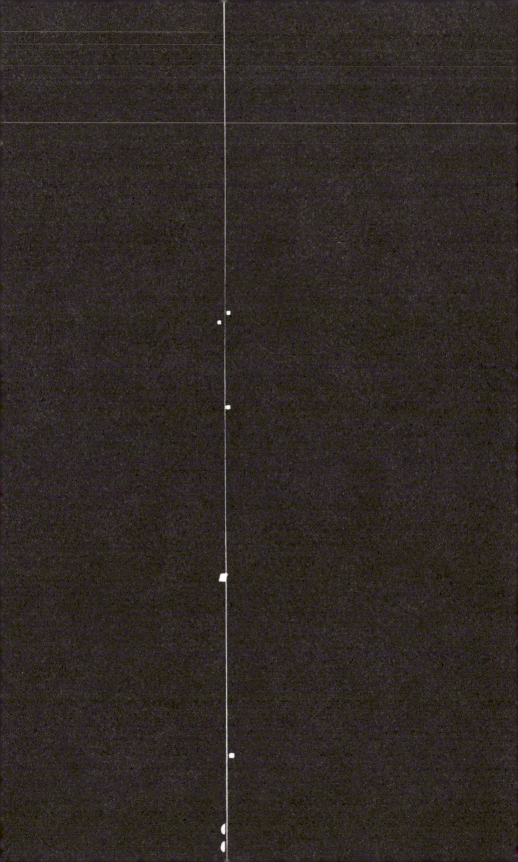

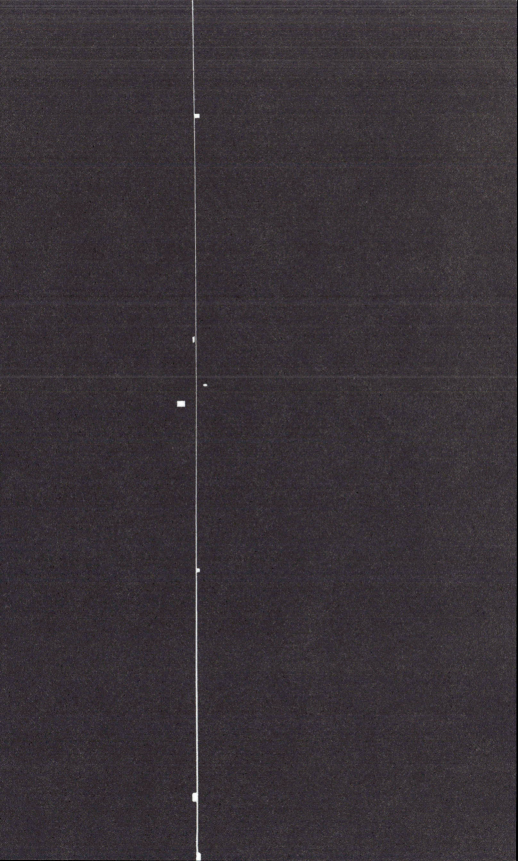

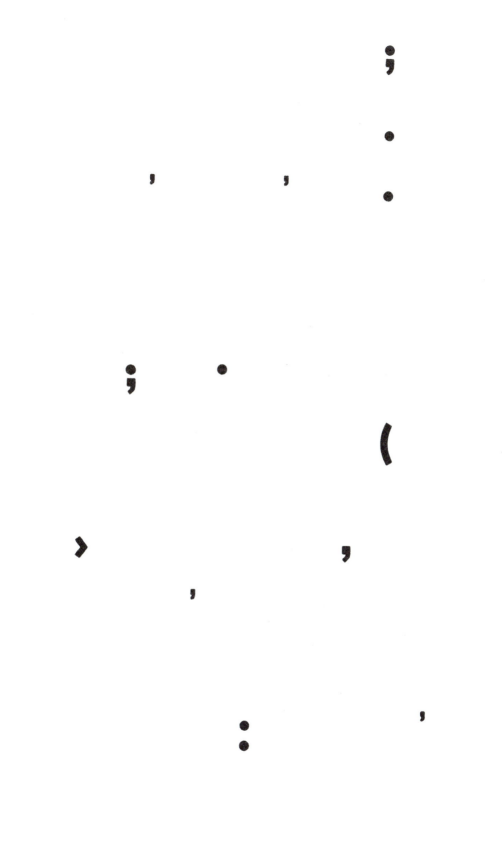

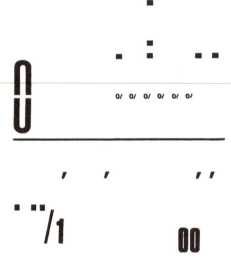

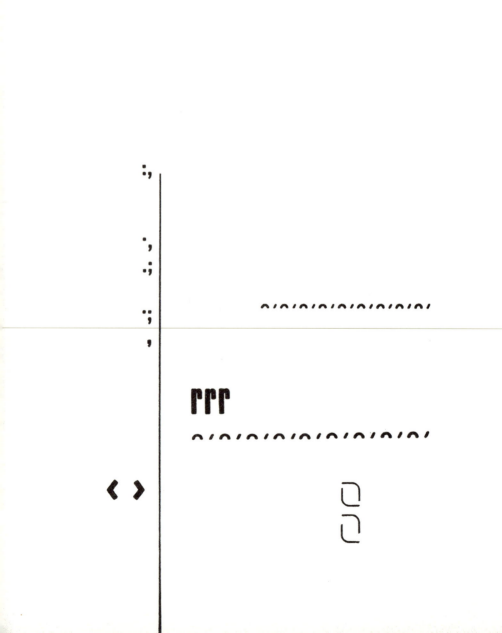

r
r

r
r

r

o

2   3   4   5   7

ɑ ɑ
ɑ ɑ

ɑ ɑ

z
z
z
z
z

e e e e e
e e e   e
e e e   e

rssstt

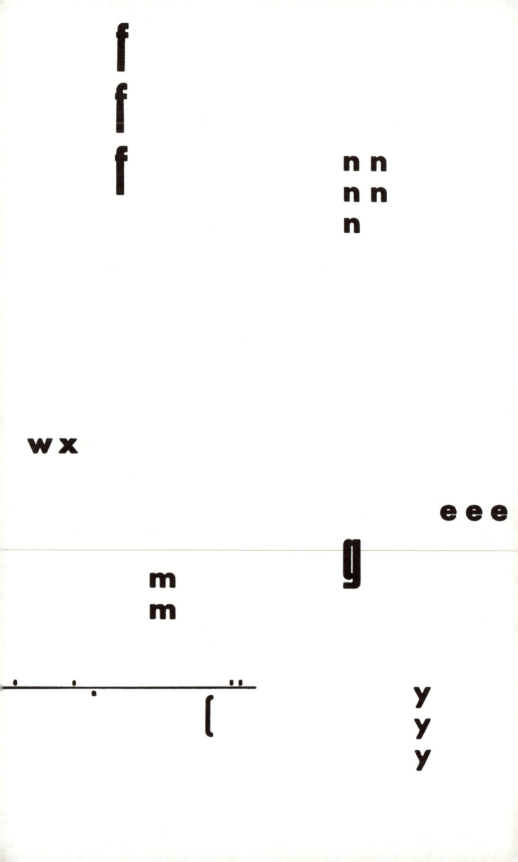

popqrr

da

da K a S

[dimora

dell'

asimmetrico

]

from

from K to S

[dwelling

of the

asymmetric

]

(1976)

TRANSLATION *Faust Pauluzzi*

pronunciando dentro di noi o formulando
a memoria le varie consonanti da K a S,
con o senza le vocali, si produce (   )
questa o quella specie di contatto con
il movimento della coscienza

Abhinavagupta

        by pronouncing within ourselves
or by voicing from memory the various
consonants from K to S, with or without
their vowel sounds, we produce (   )
this or that kind of contact with the
stirrings of consciousness

                              Abhinavagupta

49

:

via
ndante
e
viaggio

sono
soltanto
me stesso
verso
me stesso

Farid ud-din Attar

:

               pilgrim
               pilgrimage
          and
          way

          are
          but
          myself
          toward
          myself

Farid ud-din Attar

le piante (frammentarie)

                    le
                  piante
                  (   )
                frammentarie
                  del
                  palazzo
                si
                aprirono
              in
              due
            ali
          di
        fenice

    o
      di
        fagiano

52

the (fragmentary) plans

                    the
                    frag
                  mentary
            (   )
                  plans
                       of
                       the
                     palace
                  spread out
                            as
                            two
                        phoenix
                          wings

                              or
                            a
                  pheasant's

quanto nascondono

                    notte
                     di
                    nave

                altezza
                  di
              stella

            uccelli
            lucenti
          discesi
          dalle
          nubi

        svelando quanto nascondono

as much as they hide

ship
 board
  night

  star
   height

    shining
     birds
      down
       from
        the
         clouds

unveiling as much as they hide

si fermò a giocare a dadi

sulla strada che porta alla necropoli
occidentale di Eliopoli una sera
Telesforo si fermò a giocare
a dadi con il Tempo

attraversata
la valle
dei Cedri
si trovò all'alba
nel luogo sacro della
Prima Volta

alle porte del Sole

                    he stopped to play dice

on the road that leads to Heliopolis'
western necropolis one evening
 Telesphoros stopped to play
   dice with Time

        after crossing
          the valley
            of the Cedars
              he found himself at dawn
                in the sacred space of
                  the First Time

at the gates of the Sun

come un falco percuote
(frammento Ht)

"da me forte giovenca (corpo vivente)
        è state strappata la coscia"
"vi ho
presentato il fanciullo Labernas
        l'ho abbracciato e sollevato
(l'ho viziato)
                        ~~lotta contro lotta~~
(non è più mio figlio)

                come un falco percuote
come Baal nell'ora del suo furore

Dio hattico delle tempeste
                                basta
sua madre mugge come una vacca"

as a hawk strikes
(Hittite fragment)

"from me strong heifer   (living body)
            the flank was torn away"
"I have
introduced to you the boy Labernas
  I've embraced him and lifted him up
(I've spoiled him)
            struggle against struggle
(he's no longer my son)

                    as a hawk strikes
as Baal in the hour of his fury

Storm-God of Hatti
                            enough
his mother is mooing like a cow"

59

Paracelsus

passò quindi Philippus Aureolus
(Bombast von Hohenheim)   su
la tuta la carcassa della
luce (naturale)   grida
va in dialetto   le
galassie passano
per il ventre

   (atomi e
stelle)

Paracelsus

then there came Philippus Aureolus
    (Bombast von Hohenheim)   on
        his overalls the carcass of
            (natural) light he was s
            houting in dialect th
                e galaxies pass thr
                ough the belly

                (atoms
                    and stars)

pensò a

fu
chiamata
in
sogno

Koptopigia

appena
sveglia
all'alba
pensò a
una

Venere nera

she thought of

              in
            a dream
             she was
               called

             Koptopigia

              on awake
             ning
            at dawn
            she thought
          of a

black Venus

a raggiera

su
fondo
scuro
un
ciuffo
di
foglie
lunghe
a
piumino

una
piantina
a
raggiera
(radiant
halo)
di

margherite

with a radiant halo

                    on
                     a
                    dark
                background
                     a
                   tuft
                    of
                   long
                  leaves
            puff-ball like

                         a
                      tiny plant
                      with a
                      radiant
                      halo
                      (a
                      raggiera)

              of daisies

le parole germoglio

                 se
                 è
                seduto
             che subito
              si alzi
               se
               è
             in piedi
            che non
           si sieda

                     le
                   parole
                  germoglio
                  (sphoṭa)
                  chiamano
                   dai
                    libri
                   della
                    foresta
                   (āraṇyaka)

                    sprout words

                         if
                       he is
                      sitting
                   let him get
                        up now
                                 if
                              he's
                          standing
                      let him not
                           sit down

                        the
                     sprout
                     words
                   (sphoṭa)
                are calling
                  from the
                    books
                   of the
                  forest
            (āraṇyaka)

                        67

(a rovescio)

in
 una
  goccia
   di
    una
     stella
     alpina
      (se sei fortunato)
       si
        vede
         controluce
        lo
         scritto
          (a rovescio)
          di
          una
          foglia

(backwards)

                              in
                               a
                            drop
                             on
                             an
                   edelweiss
        (if you're lucky)
                   you can
                        see
                 against
              the light
                    the
              writing
        (backwards)
                   on
                    a
              leaf

i quattro petali

                           nella luce chia
rissima del mattino un fiore di
fucsia perfetto pende a si
nistra i quattro pe
tali (cardinal
i) schiu
si

a stella

the four petals

                    in
                   the
              sterling
                 light
                    of
                  morn
                     a
               perfect
        fuchsia flower
                 leans
                    to
                   the
                  left

                   its
                  four
            (cardinal)
                petals
                  open
          like a star

luce che è vento

                quella fosforescenza liquida
                in una notte d'estate una
                specie di luminosità im
            manente   le onde in
            cui acqua e vento si
            incontrano   luce
        che è vento e mo
    vimento ritmico

prima materia
                    e ne consente
        lo svolgersi

light which is wind

that   liquid   phosphorescence
on a summer's night   a sort
of   immanent   luminosity
the waves   wherein   wa
ter and wind meet   li
ght   which is   wind
and   rhythmic   mo
vement

primal matter
whose unfoldi
ng it allows

lasciarono il paradiso

lasciarono
  il luogo recinto
   per
    il bisogno
      di

    una
    pelle
  nuova in
        cui
         abitare

(Dimora dell'Asimmetrico

they left paradise

                    they left
            the enclosed space
                        for
                     need
                     of

                        a
                      new
                   skin in
                 which
               to live

        (Dwelling of the Asymmetric

un frammento

scrutando
sotto
il letto
in cerca di
dio sa che cosa

un
frammento
saltò
fino
al
cielo

e divenne luna

                    a fragment

        peering
          under
         the bed
      in search of
    god knows what

                    a
                  fragment
                  popped
                    all the way
                      up to the
                      sky

        and became moon

                    nel   tredicesimo   libro
della   Luce   dei   Tantra

                    perché Abhinavagupta nel tredice
simo libro de   lla Luce   dei
Tantra   (T   antrāloka)
avrebbe p   otuto dir
e: quan   do il ca
mpo magn   etico il
campo gr   avitazio
nale e il   campo cre
ativo coin   cidono all
ora anche coi   ncidono lo st
ato e il moto l'essere e il divenire

                    in the thirteenth book
of   the Light of Tantra

                since Abhinavagupta in the thirtee
nth book of th   e Light of Tan
tra (Tantrā   loka) could
have said: when the m
agnetic f   ield the
gravitati   onal fiel
d   and th   e creativ
e field co   incide   th
en there is   also coinci
dence   between   stasis and mov
ement   between being and becoming

                    79

mantra

fulgore/energia   (significante)
 oltre
  la
   convenzione
    (significata)
     delle
      parole (generalizzate)
       aspetto
        del linguaggio
         più
          vicino
           alla
            coscienza

  mantra

        splendor/energy   (signifier)
                                       beyond
                                         the
                                    convention
                                    (signified)
                                         of
                words   (generalized)
                                    an aspect
                                         of
                                    language
                                      closer
                                     to con
                          sciousness

alfabeto
/ albero
del
Tempo

alphabet /
tree
of Time

[1977]

TRANSLATION: *Guy Bennett*

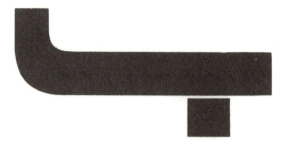

venga dal Sole
    o nasca degli aromi
        tra il verde e il secco
    questo luogo del furto

:   da Delo il fuoco nuovo

        (l'ispirazione che era
          la sostanza   )

    tutto fonde

le scintillae
ritornano

may it come from the Sun
        or be born of the scents
                mid the green and the dry
        this scene of the theft

:   from Delos the new fire

                (the inspiration that was
                    substance   )

      everything fuses

the sparkling
returns

alfabeto / albero del Tempo

si dice che Hermes
abbia portato l'alfabeto arboreo
dalla Grecia all'Egitto
e poi
di nuovo
dall'Egitto alla Grecia

                          aiutò le tre Moire
a comporre   l'alfabeto
inventò   l'astronomia
              la scala musicale

              la bilancia

e la coltivazione dell'ulivo

alphabet / tree of Time

they say that Hermes
brought the arboreal alphabet
from Greece to Egypt
then back
again
from Egypt to Greece

                              he helped the three Moirai
compose   the alphabet
he invented   astronomy
               the musical scale

               the balance

and the cultivation of the olive tree

depose
un uovo d'argento
nel grembo
dell'oscurità

(sospesa ragione
del mondo)

dell'uno   il prodigio
dell'altro   i confini

           he put
a silver egg
into the womb
of the dark

        (reason of the world
        suspended)

wonder   of the one
limits   of the other

anche le lettere dell'antico alfabeto irlandese, come quello
usato dai Druidi della Gallia (descritti da Cesare), portano il
nome degli alberi

(alberi = lettere)

ogni consonante
un mese di 28 giorni (una serie di 13 mesi)

 betulla o ulivo selvatico
 frassino di montagna
 frassino
 ontano o corniolo
 salice
 biancospino
 quercia o terebinto

 vite
 edera
 giunco o palla di neve
 sambuco o mirto

even the letters of the Old Irish alphabet, like that used by the Druids of Gaul (described by Cæsar), bore the names of trees

(trees = letters)

each consonant
a month of 28 days (a series of 13 months)

    birch or wild olive
    mountain ash
    ash
    alder or cornel
    willow
    hawthorn
    oak or terebinth

    grapevine
    ivy
    rush or snowball
    elder or myrtle

dai ramoscelli / arbusti   ai papiri

da elemento fonico   a registrazione / sostanza
                           materia / tempo
lavoro dell'uomo
segno inciso
magica derivazione

alpha da alphe (onore) alphainein (inventare)

anche   solco
aleph   bue dei Fenici

                    tempo   foglia   foglio
                    ulivo   oliva
                    lettera   frutto
                    radice (ritrovata)
                    tra i solchi
                    zappe e gerla
                    lo strumento

s'apre la terra alla storia dell''uomo

solco cuneiforme (s'alzano le gru
                    Hermes ne segue il volo a cuneo)

Ogma Volto di Sole dall'Irlanda
ripete la fatica (dall'alfabeto di Kronos
                    all'alfabeto di Heracles)

il cufico parallelo
geometrizza lo spazio (nuovo ordine)

from twigs / shrubs   to papyri

from phonic element   to recording / substance
                          matter / time
work of man
carved sign
magic derivation

alpha from alphe (honor) to alphainein (to invent)

also   furrow
aleph   ox of the Phoenecians

                time   leaf   page
                olive tree   olive
                letter   fruit
                root (rediscovered)
                between the furrows
                hoe and basket
                the instrument

the earth opens to the story of man

cuneiform furrow (cranes rise
                Hermes follows their wedge-shaped flight)

Ogma Sun-Face from Ireland
repeated the labour (from the alphabet of Chronos
                to the alphabet of Heracles)

the Kufic parallel line
geometrizes spaces (new order)

terra o roccia

s'alzano i segni sulle pareti a picco
(tavole del Tempo)
           emergono forme incise
(forma / materia / evento)
         spaziano in un non-tempo
l'acqua
l'aria smussa   incide il flusso

dai segni primari per la legge deli opposti
i cieli sono costellazioni di segni / alfabeti
le galassie vapori fonematici
che si condensano in energia del linguaggio
(itinerari / processi / novae)
         logical space
riscattato dal segno verso il simbolo

dinamo / tensione / pulsione

vitanuova

earth or rock

signs climb the cliff face
(table of Time)

carved forms emerge

(form / matter / event)

disperse in a non-time

the water
the air dulls   carves the flow

from primary signs for the law of opposites
the heavens are constellations of signs / alphabets
the galaxies phonemic vapors
condensing in linguistic energy
(itineraries / processes / novas)

logical space

sprung from the sign toward the symbol

dynamo / tension / instinct

newlife

nord   sud   est   ovest
trama del tempo
ordito dei segni

                        linea   punto   linea
                        linea   punto
                        curva   arco
                        spazio   tempo   specchio
                        parentesi che apre
                        virgola come perno
zero lucido
(stacco dall'opaco)
                        la lettera
                        il fonema
             simbolo circolare

             luce ad arco

north   south   east   west
weave of time
warp of signs

line   point   line
line   point
curve   arc
space   time   mirror
opening parenthesis
comma as hinge
clear zero
(in a break from the opaque)
the letter
the phoneme
circular symbol

arclight

dall'energia blu si estraggono coats of
arms con spirali e sequenze alfabetiche
                    emerge il bianco contemplazione
        con lettere / rituali che si trasformano in
processi / itinerari sul nero / zero del fondo
con nuove sequenze / inizio AB

                    triangoli / cerchi / semicerchi
(roteazione di) in uno spazio totale
                                        da
differenti profondità emergono lettere e signi sim-
bolici di calcoli   (operazioni / itinerari)
                    parentesi elevate a potenza
                    (aperte o chiuse)
teroemi di processi mentali che rimandano

        su fondo nero (opaco) il nero (lucido) di lettere e
numeri

coats of arms bearing alphabetic spirals
and sequences are distilled from blue energy
                    white contemplation emerges
        with   letters / rituals   that   transform   in
processes / itineraries on a black / blank background
with new sequences / beginning AB

                    triangles / circles / semicircles
(gyre of) in a total space
                                        from
different depths letters and symbolic computational
signs emerge   (operations / itineraries)
            parentheses raised to the next power
                    (open or closed)
theorems of mental processes that defer

    against an (opaque) black background the (bright)
black of letters and numbers

quando la ragione
    (dentro le viscere)

gli fece (splendida)
la loro forma
(A valore)

    i numeri
    (uno bianco uno nero)
    attraversarono in
    prospettiva

al punto dei luoghi
e degli incroci
        la traccia di
        una curva

when reason
    (in the entrails)

made (splendid)
their (valued)
form

    numbers
    (one white one black)
    crossed over in
    perspective

to the point of places
and junctions
           the trace of
           a curve

la roteazione dello spazio
organizzata per mezzo di linee / tensioni
(zero AB) (teorema degli equilibri)

spirali bianche
(sempre di lettere e numeri) su fondo blu

alcuni segni evidenziati
portati in primo piano (dinamica ulteriore)

frecce / direzione

X (incognita / moltiplicazione)

: (due punti / divisione)

=

        the gyre of space
organized by means of lines / tensions
(zero AB) (theorem of equilibria)

white spirals
(of letters and numbers always) against a blue background

some highlighted signs
shifted to the foreground (additional dynamics)

                    arrows / direction

x (unknown / multiplication)

             : (colon / division)
   =

Solone Solone
   altro non siete che fanciulli

      dall'abisso si staccherà
      dell'argilla

      bianco   nero   grigio
      poro   buco

      foro   luce   bordo

      taglio   bianco

Solon Solon
  you are but children

        clay will be torn
        from the abyss

        white   black   gray
        pore   hole

        bore   light   edge

        white   cutting

signum est res, praeter

dal canguro all'aithyia

(o come farsi scrittura)

[1981]

da una stele egizia
(XVIII dinastia)

      i cuori degli uomini
sono deboli
   hanno cessato di
         creare
la memoria non è più
  ritorno
  d'armonia   (inganna)

        non si loda più
    (non si canta)
    l'originario
c h e   p e r m e t t e

il mio segno è il senza segno

gialâl ad-dîn rûmî

quel Vicino, davanti a cui continuamente passiamo
frettolosi e distratti, vorrebbe, per contro
condurci a ritroso.
Sì, a ritroso, ma dove ?
A ciò che costituisce l'inizio.
Heidegger, *In Cammino verso il Linguaggio*

L'aithyia è un uccello mitologico, acquatico, familiare ai pescatori e ai naviganti. Se ne trovano numerosi riferimenti nei testi di antichi ornitologi, lessicografi o naturalisti, anche se non si sa esattamente a quale specie appartenga. Cormorano, cornacchia di mare, folaga, chiurlo o puffino, colimbo, gabbiano reale o tuffatore, può essere forse identificato con la cornacchia di mare (korone thalassios), che secondo antiche tradizioni era l'uomo d'altri tempi, inventore della caccia di mare, trasformatosi poi in uccello. Nidifica su promontori a picco sul mare, nelle vicinanze di porti e città, volatile terrestre ed acquatico, doppiamente anfibio (aria/acqua ed anche terra/mare): passeggia (lentamente) sulla sottile striscia (terra umida) che separa/unisce terraferma e moto ondoso.

Artemidoro, nella *Chiave dei Sogni,* racconta come sognare una cornacchia di mare presagisca una vita di navigante e una perfetta conoscenza dell'elemento marino (non navigherà mai senza punti di riferimento).

farsi scrittura è riaprirsi

all'uccello acquatico in noi

(cornacchia di mare o folaga che sia)

riscoprire la caccia

nel mare/inconscio

affiorare

nel

segno/volo che

traccia

(Hermes
   ci attraversa (preme)
     con le sue gru a stormo)   costruisce
                            graffia (ci graffia)

simbolo emerso in parola e seme

riappare l'uomo che fummo d'altri tempi, Sé rappresentato, fermato (lineare o a mappe) in scroll divinatorio: coazione liberatoria, pensiero/immagine, linguaggio/materia vivente
(codice prima dell'alba di puledri)

Occorre però sognarlo questo uccello marino, non possiamo pretendere di. Farsi scrittura è calarsi nei presagi (la Vergine Memoria ci accompagna), non si bara. È un passare dal temporale al perenne, dal personale a pura materia scrivente: operazione sacra come sanno altre civiltà, l'Oriente Zen, i curvi/geometrici miracoli delle scritture islamiche. Farsi scrittura è partecipazione alla rivelazione creatrice dell'arte, la cui funzione sacra va intesa come aprirsi a quel campo dell'esperienza umana dove il rapporto uomo/limitazione e realtà illimitata si fonde in un incontro filogenetico.

L'eradios (altro uccello acquatico mitologico) tracciava con il suo volo una via ai naviganti. Sognare l'aithyia/eradios allora è:

riconoscere
la propria natura anfibia (terra/acqua)

elemento solido su cui muoversi
liquido da cui affiorare
in cui tuffarsi

acqua/terra/aria
    volo (direzione/allargamento di)
    traccia
     sulla sottile striscia (breve è il Tempo)
    solco e impronta

  è ritrovare il proprio destino di navigante
      nell'esperienza/espressione

           in
        out
             ala
      onda
   vento
     ombra
tra Rupi Mobili

(non navigare senza punti di riferimento). Che sono
farsi segno / parola / verbo, lasciare che il Progetto senza
Volto (il non detto) affiori, ritrovare Tavole di significato
e senso (vita). Compiere la metamorfosi dal canguro
al pellicano, all'aithyia: noi marsupiali, grembo di noi
stessi / realtà / scontro / intensità / trasformazione.   Se   il
nutrimento non si trova, strapparlo dalle viscere

unghia / stilo / penna / gesto
(incidere / segnare)

       volare
dalla   città   temporale

via
dal porto (arco al mare)

        da
    rupe a rupe

terra umida / terraferma / moto ondoso

       Se la scrittura è drammatizzazione del
linguaggio che duplica in termini visuali, conformandosi
ad un codice linguistico, le infinite variazioni che si possono
determinare in tale visualizzazione superano il concetto di
duplicazione ed evidenziano sfaccettature di codici diversi
(ritmopersonali / psicodinamici) secondo i livelli culturali
di cui sono l'espressione.

       In Islam la scrittura è un assoluto,
l'Assoluto: secoli fa un calligrafo arabo affermava che è
la punta della penna ciò che differenzia culture diverse.
Come calligrafi gli Arabi non sono mai stati superati,
solo i Cinesi in modo diverso, possono essere considerati
loro pari. Popoli nomadi e dalle tradizioni orali, gli
Arabi erano conosciuti nell'antichità come nazione di
poeti; si posero in modo determinante il problema della
scrittura solo dopo la scomparsa del Profeta, quando
dovettero trascrivere i sacri testi del Corano, dando
così origine alla miracolosa fioritura di calligrafi. Senza

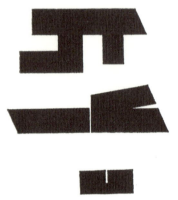

una precedente tradizione scritta, fantasia e immaginazione
si espressero liberamente; la loro natura di poeti affiora in
ogni segno curvo o allungato fino al limite massimo della tensione o
matematicamente proporzionato
: scrittura e illuminazione sono strettamente legate.

      Logica e immaginazione si combinano nell'arte
calligrafica islamica. Per esprimere questo duplice concetto
anzi gli Arabi hanno una sola parola *al-Adab*, che indica
l'approccio logico e quello immaginativo congiunti, due
metodi che non si sarebbero mai dovuti separare, come
affermano.

      (La nazione dei poeti è infatti anche la nazione
degli scienziati medievali, che tramandarono / elaborarono
il pensiero matematico greco) (*algebra* poi deriva dall'arabo
al-giabr, la reunione delle parti.)

Nella scrittura islamica si notano forme geometriche che si
combinano in aperti arabeschi, realizzando una perfezione
statica di completezza e uno splendore dinamico dalle
infinite vibrazioni.

      Nata come espressione di un sacro determinato
(il Corano), questa scrittura raggiunge un assoluto che
trascende.

      Per i calligrafi arabi la loro arte è geometria
dello spirito espressa attraverso il corpo.

      I Giapponesi, invece, per indicare una
persona piena di grazia, dicono che ha una bella scrittura.
Nel loro vocabolario esiste una parola che esprime un
concetto percepito diviso, o ancora confusamente, da noi
occidentali. È una delle parole giapponesi più semplici ed
ambigue (quasi un soffio): *ma,* il cui equivalente manca
nel nostro vocabolario e che può aiutarci a comprendere il
valore di quella dimensione della scrittura che chiameremo
organizzazione nello Spazio, in cui i segni sono registrazione
del Tempo.

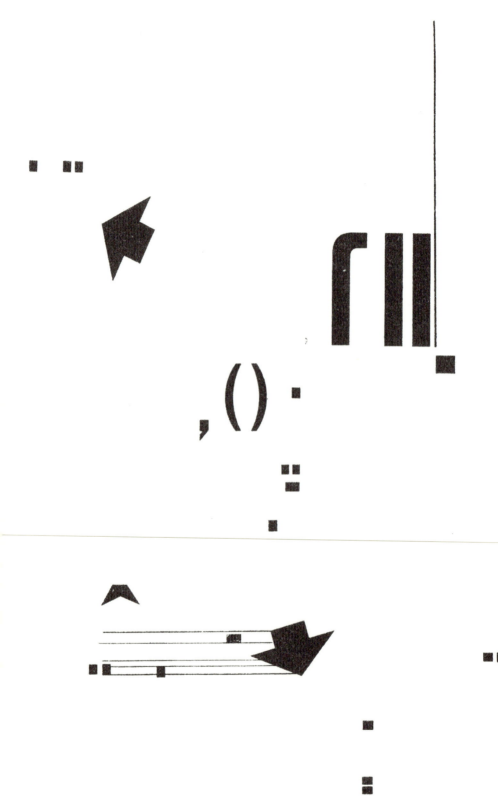

ma significa
quella distanza naturale
tra
due o più cose
esistenti in un continuum

ma
è cio che divide il mondo

è il modo di esprimere il momento
del movimento

ma è
quella unità strutturale
per lo spazio vivente

è
il luogo
dove
si vive la vita

e ancora
:
ma
è quel senso
di   sottile   equilibrio   dello   spazio/tempo
come
noi lo sperimentiamo
unito
fuso

(non separato

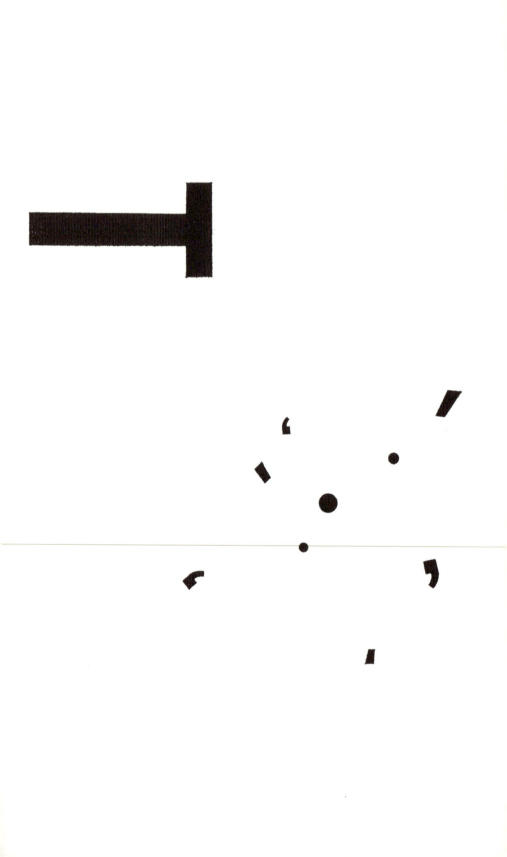

Tenendo presente la fantasia / immaginazione delle scritture islamiche e la vibrazione orientale dello spazio, da cui emerge la drammatizzazione della scrittura, vediamo ora che cosa avviene nel nostro diverso ambito culturale, in cui da Mallarmé, Apollinaire, via Futurismo, in questa seconda metà del secolo, e sopratutto negli ultimi venti anni, la scruttura visuale ha avuto un largo sviluppo, diventando anche un fenomeno di moda, con relative limitazioni.
(Non basta un rapporto esterno con gli acrostici (rifarsi *a* non ha radici): occorre che avvenga una stessa evoluzione interna.)

Nella cultura occidentale tempo, spazio, logica e immaginazione   sono concetti separati, ma che nella struttura profonda dell'essere conservano pulsioni indivise. Due termini nel nostro vocabolario possono farci risalire a quella struttura profonda

: *momento*

movimento

in cui l'attimo / scorrere del tempo si realizza in un fluire spaziale

(dal latino *momentum*

contrazione di *movimentum*

da *movere*

radice *meu*

, spostarsi)

Per logica e immaginazione, invece, anche se etimologicamente non hanno alcun contatto, dobbiamo risalire ai Presocratici, quando *mito* e *logos* non si confrontavano ancora (Parmenide, nel frammento 8, usa mito e logos nello stesso senso).

Mito significa racconto, parola che dice: dimora dell'immaginario, logos per eccellenza. Già con Platone mito e logos hanno perduto la loro essenza originaria.

L'immaginazione è pulsione profonda da riattivarsi in questa nostra cultura dominata dal logos, in cui si riconosce solo alla fantasia (confusa spesso con l'immaginazione) capacità combinatoria con funzione liberante.

Dal Romanticismo alla psicoanalisi, il mondo delle immagini ha subito un continuo processo di rivalutazione. Nel suo saggio pubblicato sulla rivista Spring (1971), *Exploration of the Imaginal,* Gilbert Durand afferma anzi che nel prossimo secolo i contenuti dell'inconscio (le immagini) saranno uno dei più importanti campi di indagine.

Attualmente però siamo inflazionati sia dalle immagini dei mass media, sia da un logos che non controlla, a cui sfuggono i fili della trama.

L'immaginazione/pulsione del Progetto senza Volto è ancora velata.

In una intervista su Repubblica (maggio 1979) Roland Barthes notava che « le civiltà avanzate hanno un enorme consumo di immagini, e un consumo minimo di credenze. Le società liberali sono dominate da un immaginario generalizzato, quale non è mai esistito al mondo. Persino nella Chiesa Cattolica l'immaginario è intatto, ma le credenze sono indebolite ».

Gli uomini si muovono a caso
    gli dei si sottraggono
        manca quel gradiente/piano inclinato
      che permette/indirizza lo sfogo dell'energia
      in una direzione positiva trasformatrice.
        Immagini condizionanti esterne
            ingorgano
          rendono distruttivi
        (caos che conosciamo).

In questa situazione la scrittura visuale si propone come gradiente interno/invito/graduale pendenza su cui indirizzare la ricerca di quel Progetto Velato
per
   registrare
      i (minimi) (segno/impronta/solco)
        della conflagrazione
          o aprirsi
            alla (dinamica) quiete
              che custodisce il non detto

senza Corano da tramandare
tentare il diverso sacro (radice/vita)
                             oltrepassare
                      sgomento smarrimento
               (resistenze)
          rifarsi al campo in cui
      gli dei non si sottraggono

Nel caso della calligrafia islamica, come si è detto, l'artista copia un testo dato: si svela un significato, appare una immagine che si trasforma in formula divina. La scrittura visuale, invece, non si rifà ad alcun testo, e diventa (indipendentemente dall'humus da cui emerge e dai mezzi tecnici usati) essa stessa *il testo,* che si sacralizza in quanto testimonia una espressione di vita/dramma/gesto altrimenti non comunicabile. Non è espressione di un dato divino, ma proprio per la carenza di questa struttura dello spirito (il sacro), ne diventa una obliqua (inconscia) manifestazione. Dramma/gesto che non si è fatto ancora rituale (assicurazione di identità), ma che nella individuale *coazione a* lo presuppone:

```
                                    traccio
                          segno
              organizzo
                                    affioro
                    (
                    eco di un coro
                                    ancora sommerso
                                                            )
    )
      radice
        del sacro senza        (
                          simbolo
                    della nostra registrazione


                          )
```

Se potrebbero trovare piuttosto punti di contatto tra
la scrittura visuale e quella cinese, la cui essenza è
dominata dal rapporto azione / parola viva. Per i Cinesi
ogni espressione della loro lingua (scritta o parlata) deve
raffigurare il loro pensiero:

esprimere / raffigurare

non significa semplicemente evocare

ma suscitare / realizzare

(pulsione degli emblemi).

          Il riappropriarsi della scrittura a fini
creativi, nel nostro mondo occidentale con una
diversa tradizione scritta, è stato determinato sia dalla
rivalutazione del significante in rapporto al significato, sia
della ricerca dell'individuale / espressione, come reazione
alla massificazione del mezzo comunicante alienato.
La scrittura visuale rientra così sia nel fenomeno della
rivalutazione dell'immagine, sia in quello di reazione
all'immaginario generalizzato. Ma nel momento stesso in

cui si ripropone come *altro* alla generalizzazione di massa, per limitazione culturale (esistenziale) riproduce (fa emergere) un altro immaginario generalizzato.

Si è prodotta una reazione, diciamo così, semiologica, una quantità di analisi (anatomia) con debole (molto debole) struttura portante. Si denunciano i meccanismi di condizionamento, ma spesso si rimane invischiati in sberleffi, con accostamenti a volte goliardici, a volte ammiccanti (pretesa di).

Manca il respiro profondo del Briccone / Fool
                           dalla Rupe del Capovolto:
non è emersa
la forza pulsante di alcuna credenza
che è coscienza di tutte le crisi / ondate che
bisogna registrare nel profondo dell'essere
per attraversare
      un germe ancora intatto
il generalizzato

                       via da Troia
              da Bisanzio
                 da Nagasaki
da Leningrado
              da Varsavia
        dai bunker di Berlino
                           fuoco
                      o barcone che sia
      fiamme
          riserva
ghetto

    o
      gulag

         (dramma di farsi vivi

Contrapposto però all'immaginario generalizzato (stimolo esterno), parallelamente agisce, sotterraneo, l'immaginario pulsione trasformatrice (stimolo interno), in cui il dramma delle carenze e delle possibilità si attua e si esprime.
Come risposta a questo stimolo interno, dalla scrittura / segno si passa alla scrittura / simbolo, con tutte le implicazioni che il termine comporta

(dal lat. *symbŏlum*
gr. *sýmbolon, symbállō* 'metto insieme'
da *syn-* 'con' e *ballō* 'getto')

Simbolo inteso quindi come vaso alchemico, in cui gli elementi limitati utilizzati dalla zone conscia si combinano per pulsione inconscia tra di loro
superando il definibile / limitazione e
combinandosi in Opus / illimitato.

Affiora così
il non detto / Progetto senza Volto che si
realizza nel momento stesso della trasformazione
e in ogni altro momento
in cui lo si sperimenta.

Reazione quindi a catena
nata dall'operazione alchemica
(azione che la determina)
e
che si riproduce
ogni volta che in tempi diversi
oggetti diversi la fronteggiano.

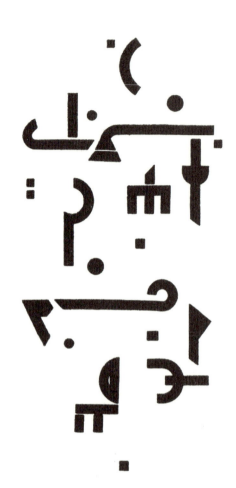

Ma se si osserva
il fenomeno da una prospettiva diversa
(punto di vista molto più distante),   si può anche accen-
nare a una metafisica definizione di Heidegger, da
Che Cosa Significa Pensare ? :

nella sua
marcia verso ciò che si sottrae
l'uomo è un segno.

Nel farsi scrittura, allora, può avvenire che la donna / l'uomo
si facciano segno del non detto, diminuendo così la distanza
con ciò che si sottrae.

E si possono concludere questi
appunti incompleti (accenni a) con un'altra citazione,
sempre da Heidegger (*In Cammino verso il Linguaggio*):

il pensare non è mezzo per conoscere
il pensare traccia solchi nel campo dell'essere.

LAPSUS ICAR

la donna
/ segno / scrittura
l'uomo

si fanno solco
di quel campo

in
cui
il non detto
che si sottrae

rivela
'quel profumo di grano'
percepito da Nietzsche
in una notta d'estate
del 1875

(o
intorno a)

profumo di nutrimento   spiga   e seme

roma 1979/80

from
the kangaroo
to the aithyia
[or how
to become
writing
]

[1981]

TRANSLATION: *Guy Bennett*

from an Egyptian stele

(Dynasty XVIII)

men's hearts
are weak
they have ceased
creating
memory is no longer
return
of harmony   (it deceives)

we no longer praise
(nor sing)
the original
w h i c h   e n a b l e s

my sign is signlessness

jalāl ad-dīn muhammad rūmī

While the nearness we constantly rush past, hurried and distracted,
would rather bring us back.
Back yes, but where?
To what comes at the beginning.
                                    – Heidegger, from *On The Way to Language*

The aithyia is a mythological aquatic bird familiar to fishermen and navigators. There are many references to them in ancient ornithological and lexicographic texts, as well as in works of natural history, even if it is not exactly clear to which species they belonged. Cormorant, sea crow, coot, curlew or puffin, loon, herring or diving gull, it can be identified with the sea crow (*korone thalassios*) which, according to ancient traditions, was the man of former times and the inventor of spearfishing, who was later changed into a bird. Nesting on sheer coastal promontories near ports and cities, this terrestrial and aquatic bird is doubly amphibious (air/water and also land and sea): it walks (slowly) on the thin strip (damp earth) that separates/unites dry land and ocean swell.

In the *The Interpretation of Dreams,* Artemidorus explains that dreaming of a sea crow presages a navigator's life and a perfect knowledge of the sea (you can never navigate without points of reference).

to become writing is to open oneself again
to the aquatic bird within us
(be it sea crow or coot)
to rediscover spearfishing
in the sea/unconscious
to surface
in the
sign/flight that
draws

(Hermes
   crosses here (presses)
      with his swarm of cranes)   builds
                  scratches (scratches us)

symbol emerged in word and sign

the man of former times that we once were reappears, his Self represented, fixed (linear or by map) on a divinatory scroll: liberating duress, thought/image, living language/material (first code from the dawn of the stallions)

But we must dream that sea bird, we cannot pretend to. To become writing is to fall into premonitions (Virgin Memory accompanies us), not to cheat oneself. It is a passing from the temporal to the eternal, from the personal to pure writing matter: it is a sacred operation as other civilizations know, the Zen Orient, the curves/geometric miracles of Islamic scripts. To become writing is to participate in the creative revelation of art, whose sacred function must be understood as opening oneself to that field of human experience in which the relationship man/limitation and unlimited reality are fused in a phylogenetic encounter.

The eradios (another mythological aquatic bird) in its flight charted a path for navigators. Dreaming the aithyia/eradios is thus:

> to recognize
> one's own amphibious nature
> (earth/water)

> solid element on which to move
> liquid element out of which to emerge
> into which to dive

water/earth/air
flight (direction/widening of)
trace
on the thin strip (Time is short)
wake and imprint

is to recover one's own destiny as a navigator
in experience/expression

in

out

wing

wave

wind

shadow

between Moving Cliffs

(to not navigate without points of reference). That they are to become sign / word / verb, to allow that the Project without a Face (the unsaid) surface, to recover Tables of meaning and sense (life). To complete the metamorphosis from the kangaroo to the pelican, to the aithyia: we marsupials, womb to ourselves / reality / conflict / intensity / transformation. If nou-rishment cannot be found, to tear it from our entrails

fingernail / stylus / pen / gesture

(to engrave / to mark)

to fly

from the temporal city

through

the port (archway to the sea)

from

cliff to cliff

damp earth / dry land / ocean swell

If writing is the dramatization of language which duplicates in visual terms, in compliance with a linguistic code, the infinite variations that can be determined in such visualization exceed the concept of duplication and highlight facets of diverse codes (personal rhythms / psychodynamic) according to the cultural levels of which they are an expression.

In Islam writing is an absolute, the Absolute: centuries ago an Arab calligrapher affirmed that the various cultures are distinguished by the tips of their pens. As calligraphers the Arabs have never been outdone, only the Chinese, in a different way, can be considered their equals. A nomadic people of oral traditions, the Arabs were known in Antiquity as a nation of poets; the problem of writing was only posed decisively after the disappearance of the Prophet, when they had to transcribe the sacred texts of the Qur'an, thus giving rise to the miraculous flowering of calligraphers. Without a pre-existing written tradition,

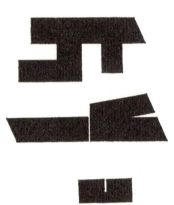

fantasy and imagination could be expressed freely; their poetic nature surfaced in every sign, whether curved or elongated to the limit of maximal tension or mathematically proportioned : writing and illumination are closely related.

Logic and imagination are combined in Islamic calligraphic art. Indeed, to express this double concept the Arabs have a single word *al-Adab,* which indicates both the logical and imaginative approach combined, two methods which never should have been separated, as they affirm.

(The nation of poets is in fact also the nation of medieval sciences, that handed down/expanded on Greek mathematical thought) (*algebra* thus is derived from the Arabic *al-jabr,* the reunion of parts.)

In Islamic writing we note geometric forms combined in open arabesques, realizing a static perfection of completion and a dynamic splendor from infinite vibrations.

Born as the expression of a sacred given (the Qur'an), this writing attains a absolute which it transcends.

The Arab calligraphers see their art as the geometry of the spirit expressed through the body.

On the other hand, to indicate a graceful person the Japanese say that he or she has a beautiful writing. In their vocabulary there is a word that expresses a concept perceived as split, or rather confusedly, by we Westerners. It is one of the most simple and ambiguous Japanese words (almost a breath): *ma,* whose equivalent is lacking in our vocabulary and which can help us understand the value of that dimension of writing that we shall call *organization in Space,* in which signs are the recording of Time.

ma signifies
that natural distance
between
two or more things
existing in a continuum

ma
is that which divides the world

it is the way to express the moment
of movement

ma is
that structural unit
for living space

it is
the place
in which
life is lived

and also
:
ma
is that sense
of   subtle   balance   of space / time
as
we experience it
united
fused

(not separated

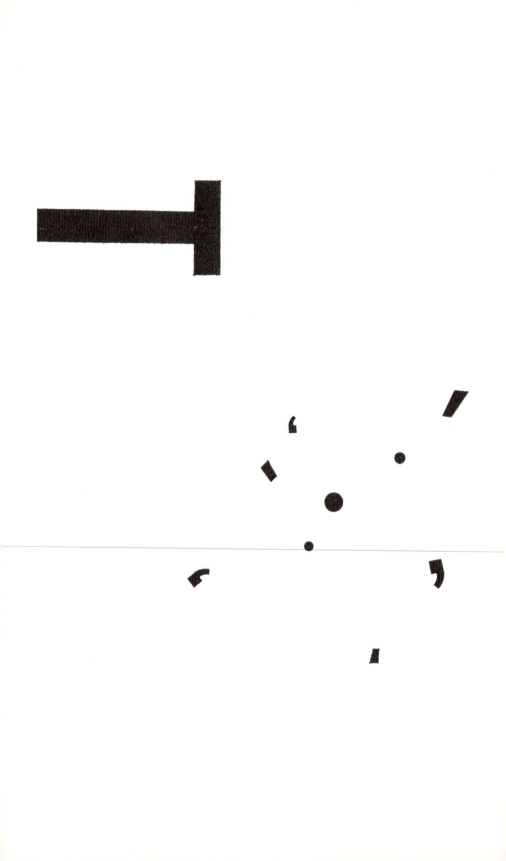

Bearing in mind the fantasy/imagination of Islamic scripts and the Asian vibration of space, from which the dramatization of writing emerges, we now see what happens in our own cultural sphere in which, from Mallarmé and Apollinaire, through Futurism, in this second half of the century and especially in the last twenty years, visual writing has developed significantly, to the point of becoming a fashion phenomenon, with relative restrictions.

(An external relationship with acrostics is not enough (to refer *to* has no roots): an identical internal evolution must take place.)

In western culture time, space, logic, and imagination are separate concepts, but in the deep structure of being they maintain undivided impulses. Two terms of our vocabulary can make us go back to that deep structure

: *moment*

movement

in which the instant/passing of time is realized in a spatial flow

(from the Latin *momentum*

contraction of *movimentum*

from *movere*

root *meu*

, to be displaced)

For logic and imagination, on the other hand, though they be unrelated etymologically, we must go back to the Presocratics, when *myth* and *logos* were not yet competing with one another (Parmenides, in the eighth fragment, uses myth and logos in the same sense).

Myth means story, a word that says: dwelling of the imaginary, logos par excellence. Already with Plato myth and logos have lost their original essence.

We must revive the profound impulse of the imagination in our logos-dominated culture, in which only fantasy (often confused with imagination) is seen as having liberating, combinatorial powers.

From Romanticism to psychoanalysis, the world of images has been under continuous reassessment. In his essay "Exploration of the Imaginal," published in the journal *Spring* in 1971, Gilbert Durand declares that in the coming century the contents of the unconscious (images) will constitute one of the most important fields of inquiry.
Currently however we are saturated either by images from mass media or by a logos that cannot control or retain the threads of the plot.
The imagination / impulse of the Project without a Face is still veiled.

In an interview that appeared in *Repubblica* in May 1979, Roland Barthes observed that "advanced civilizations have
a tremendous consumption of images, and a minimal consumption of beliefs. Liberal societies are dominated by a generalized imagination, which was previously unknown. Even in the Catholic Church the imagination remains intact, though beliefs have grown weaker."

Men move about aimlessly
          the gods withdraw
                    there is no inclined gradient / plain
                    to allow / direct the flow of energy
               in a positive, transformative direction.
                    External conditioning images
                              block
                    render destructive
                    (familiar chaos).

In this context visual writing could well act as an internal gradient/invitation/gradual slope on which to direct research into the Veiled Project

to

  register

    the (minimal) dramas (sign/imprint/furrow)

      of the conflagration

        or be opened

          to the (dynamic) calm

            that safeguards the unsaid

with no Qur'an to hand down
to attempt the alter-sacred (root/life)

                  to go beyond

                dismay confusion

             (resistance)

         to refer to the field in which

     the gods do not withdraw

In the case of Islamic calligraphy, as mentioned above, the artist copies a given text: a meaning is revealed, an image appears and is transformed into a divine formula. On the contrary, visual writing does not reproduce any text; independently of the fertile ground from which it emerges as well as of the technical means used, it itself becomes *the text,* which is sacralized since it bears witness to an otherwise incommunicable expression of life/drama/gesture. It is not an expression of any divine given, but precisely because of the lack of any spiritual framework (the sacred), it becomes an oblique (unconscious) manifestation of it. Drama/gesture not yet become ritual (assurance of identity), but which in the individual *compulsion to* presupposes it:

                                        I mark
                        sign
        organize
                                        surface
                (
                        echo of a chorus
                                still submerged
)
)
    root
        of the sacred without   (
                                symbol
                        of our registration

)

One might instead find points of contact between visual
writing and Chinese characters, whose essence is dominated
by the relationship action/living word. For the Chinese
each expression of their language (written or spoken) must
represent their thought:
                                        to express/represent
                                does not simply mean to evoke
                                        but engender/realize
(impulse of emblems).

                    In the West with its different written
tradition, the reappropriation of writing for creative
purposes has been determined either by the reassessment of
the signifier in relation to the signified, or by research of the
individual/expression in reaction to the massification of the
alienated means of communication. Visual writing is thus
part of the phenomenon of the reassessment of the image,
or that of reaction to the generalized imagination. But at the

very moment it again arises as *other* to mass generalization,
as a result of (existential) cultural limitation it reproduces
(brings to light) another generalized imagination.
There is a reaction, a semiological one let us say, a number
of analyses (anatomy) with weak (very weak) load-bearing
structures. Conditioning mechanisms are revealed, but are
often caught making faces approaching either the goliardic
or the flirtatious (claiming to be).
We lack the deep breath of the Rogue / Fool
                              from the Rock of the Inverted:
still await
the pulsating force of any belief
that is awareness of all crises / surges that
need be recorded in the depths of being
in order to pass through
   a still intact seed
the generalized

                                        away from Troy
                    from Byzantium
                              from Nagasaki
from Leningrad
                         from Warsaw
           from the bunkers of Berlin
                                             fire
                                       or chance pontoon
              flame
                    reservation
ghetto

         or
           gulag

                    (drama of becoming living

Yet in opposition to the generalized imagination
(external stimulus), subterranean, the transforming impulse
imagination   (internal stimulus), in which the drama of
deficiencies and possibilities is actualized and expressed,
acts in parallel.
In response to this internal stimulus, we go from writing / sign
to writing / symbol, with all of the implications the term
includes

(from Latin *symbŏlum*
Greek *sýmbolon, symbállō* "I put together"
from *syn-* "with" and *ballō* "I throw").

Symbol therefore meaning alchemical vessel, in which the
limited elements used by the conscious region combine with
one another through unconscious impulse
exceeding the definable / limitation and
combining into Opus / unlimited.

Thus surfaces
the unsaid / Project without a Face that is
realized   at   the   very   moment   of   transformation
and at every other moment
in which it is experienced.

Chain reaction therefore
born of the alchemical operation
(action which determines it)
and
which is reproduced
each time that at different moments
different objects face it.

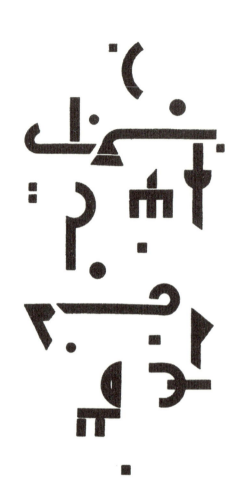

But if the phenomenon
is observed from a different perspective
(a much more distant point of view),   we can also evoke
a metaphysical definition by Heidegger, from
What is Called Thinking? :

As he
draws towards what withdraws,
man is a sign.

In the fact of becoming writing, then, it can happen that
woman / man become a sign of the unsaid, thus reducing the
distance with what withdraws.

And if these incomplete notes
(signs to) can be concluded with another quotation, again
from Heidegger (*On the Way to Language*):

Thinking is not a means to gain knowledge.
Thinking cuts furrows into the soil of Being.

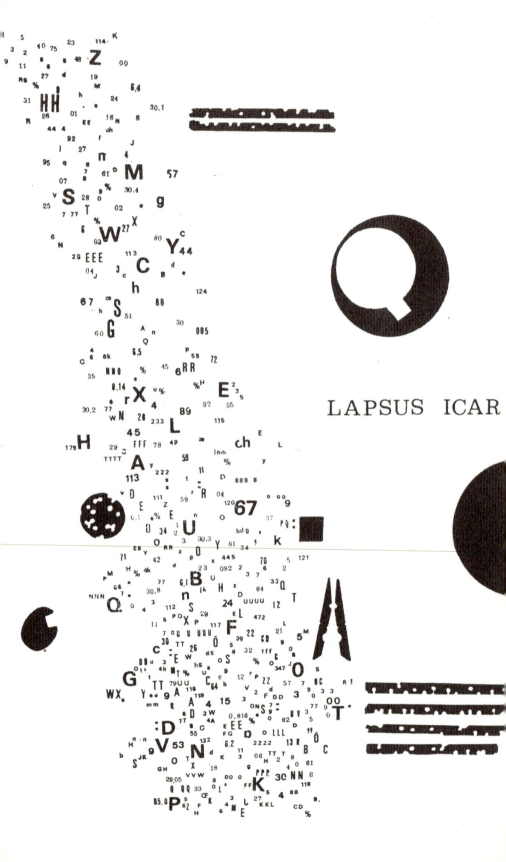

LAPSUS ICAR

woman
/ sign / writing
man

become furrow
of that field

in
which
the unsaid
that withdraws

reveals
that "fragrance like a wheatfield"
perceived by Nietzsche
one summer night
in 1875

(or
thereabouts)

fragrance of nourishment   stalk   and seed

rome 1979/80

da

clessidra :
il
ritmo
delle
tracce

[1992]

perché l'ascolto non sia perduto
emergono dalla memoria, come respiro ed onda
il ritmo delle tracce, il mantello del viandante

: solleva la poesia l'invisibile cortina
sull'enigma della Sfinge

*: in Oriente, da giochi complessi
fondati sull'astronomia si sviluppò
una specie di stenografia che di-
ventò poi l'alfabeto.*

— SANTILLANA,
Il Mulino d'Amleto

clessidra

una smagliatura di sabbia
trattiene il bandolo
dall'asfalto
del tempo

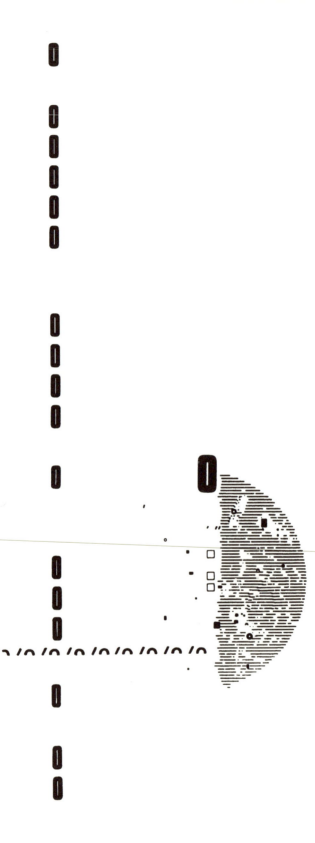

creazione illimitata

attraversando
il come
per discontinuità e
fluttuazione

:
né puro inizio
                    né pura fine   ma
        eterno
              (irreversibile)
                          mutare

nel
suo avanzare
la freccia
del
Tempo
com
pensa
quel
che
la
scia
cader
e

,

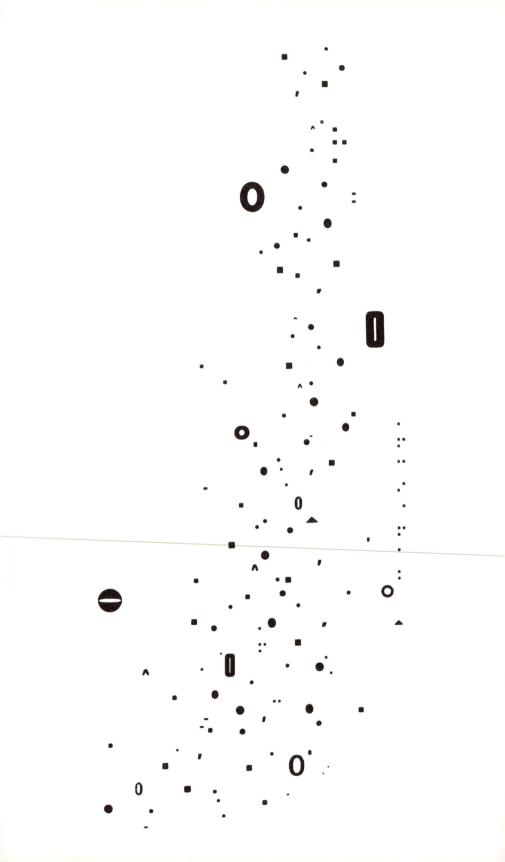

riangolare gli assi

nella veglia
delle costellazioni
una nube
di probabilità
(senza
equazioni)

:

squarta il
lutto
il
pre
valere
dell'
and
ar
e

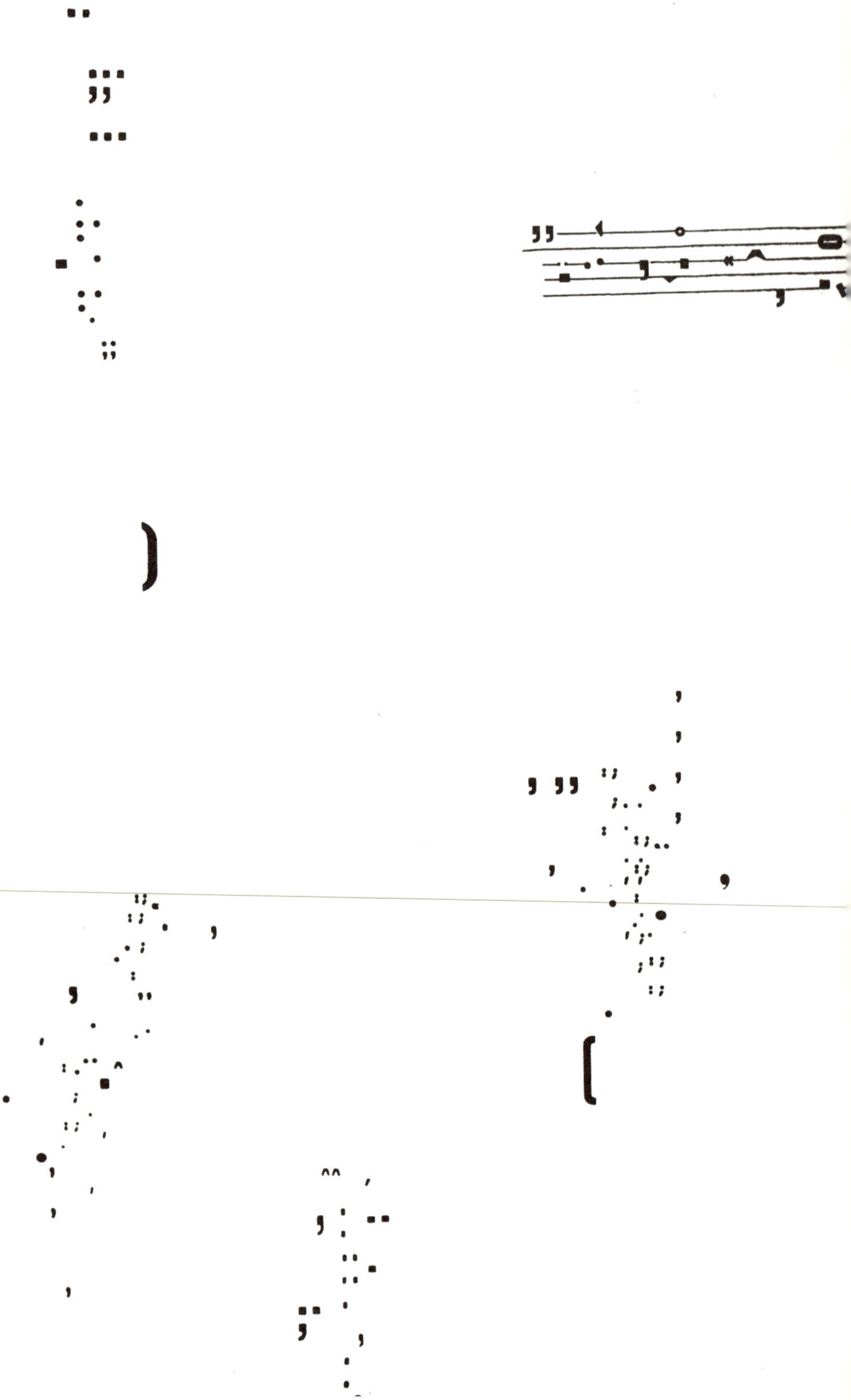

incontro

la traversata fu
    tormentosa e
        densa di
            scricchiolii

                nelle parole
            che incontra
              non trova
                  che frammenti

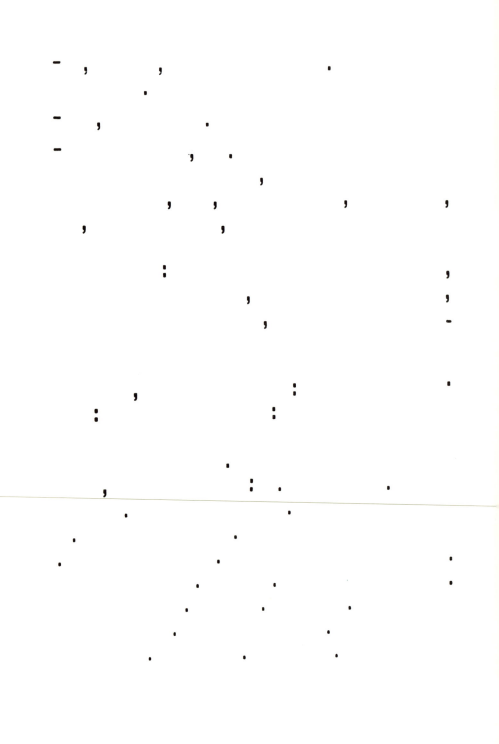

mare

nel
fondo
  degli abissi
        muta è la corrente
      e nera
             strappata è
              la rete dei ricordi
        :
    un groviglio
  di nord
      est
        sud
          ovest
              senza
           più
        sestante

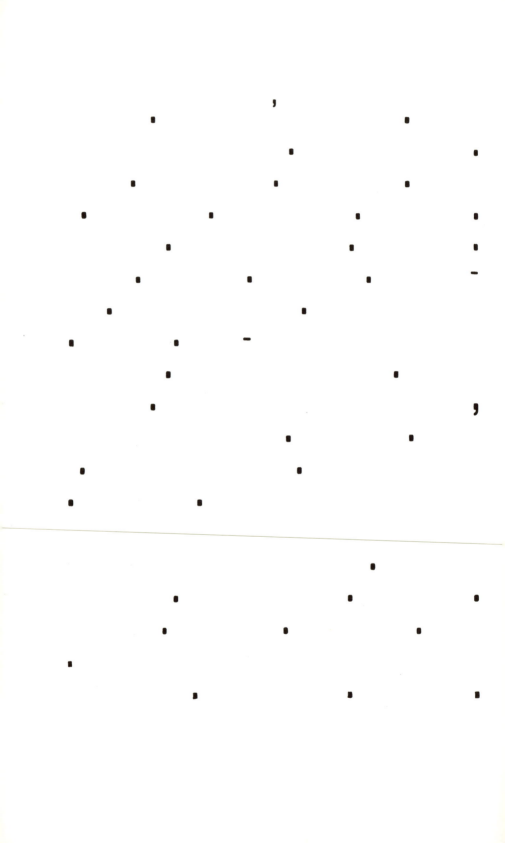

on/of

                              una bottiglia gettata
                         nel mare del
                    futuro
fluttua
      tra i flutti di
                    correnti
                      senza rotte

                  nella notte
           una forma
                 cerca
                    l'orizzonte

                     :

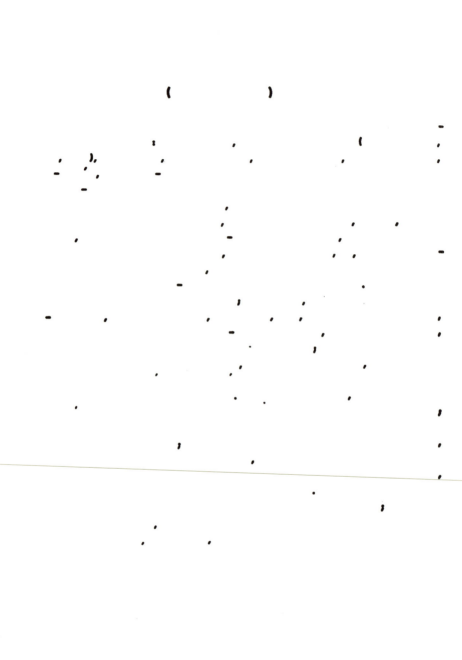

(un groviglio)

                                        nel
                                    nonlibro
                                segreto
                            della
                    mente
        un impaccio
            (un groviglio)
                di memorie

                                    compagne
                                        di fughe
                                            fuochi fatui   e

            zaffiri
        sprezzati
            dal
                tempo

con i resti

        nel
   l'
atrio
di
  Keplero
     il lutto della ringhiera
        e
            con i resti ne fece un ideogramma

sì che

l'ovatta di una
                  nuvola
si sfrangia
        sì che
      la luna

un attimo
             risplenda
al suo passagio
         sfioccato
                 dal vento

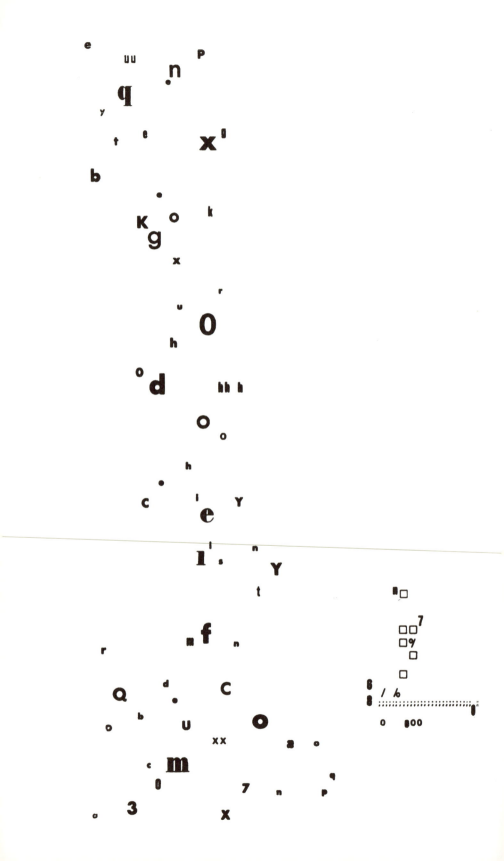

hieros gamos

noi due andare
    né qui   né ora
        (ovunque   o mai)

                senza esordio   o stampo
        (senza gestazione

)

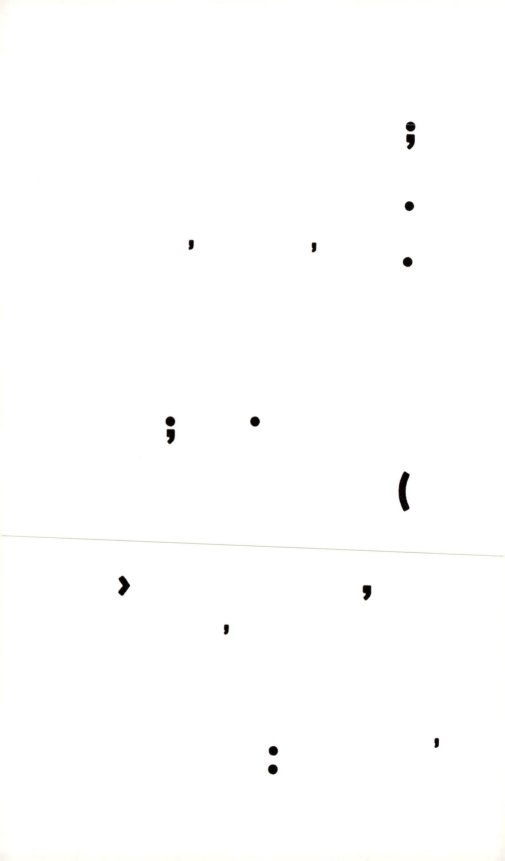

sì come nelle coppe l'acqua scorre attraverso
il filo di lana dalla più piena alla più vuota
sarebbe pur bello, o Glaucone,
se la sapienza fosse fatta in modo da scorrere
attraverso le lettere dell'alfabeto
(gocce i frammenti)

— PLATONE, *Simposio*

from

hourglass:
　　the rhythm
　　　　　of
　　traces

[1992]

TRANSLATION: *Guy Bennett*

so that listening not be lost
the rhythm of traces, the wayfarer's cloak emerge
from memory, like breath and wave

: poetry raises the invisible curtain
on the enigma of the Sphinx

: in the East, out of complicated games based on astronomy, there developed a kind of shorthand which became the alphabet.

— SANTILLANA,
Hamlet's Mill

hourglass

a wrinkle of sand
keeps the flow
from the asphalt
of time

limitless creation

crossing
the as
through discontinuity and
fluctuation

   :

neither pure beginning
                   nor pure end   but
      eternal
         (irreversible)
                change

the arrow
of
Time
com
pensates
what
its
trail
lets
fal
l

,

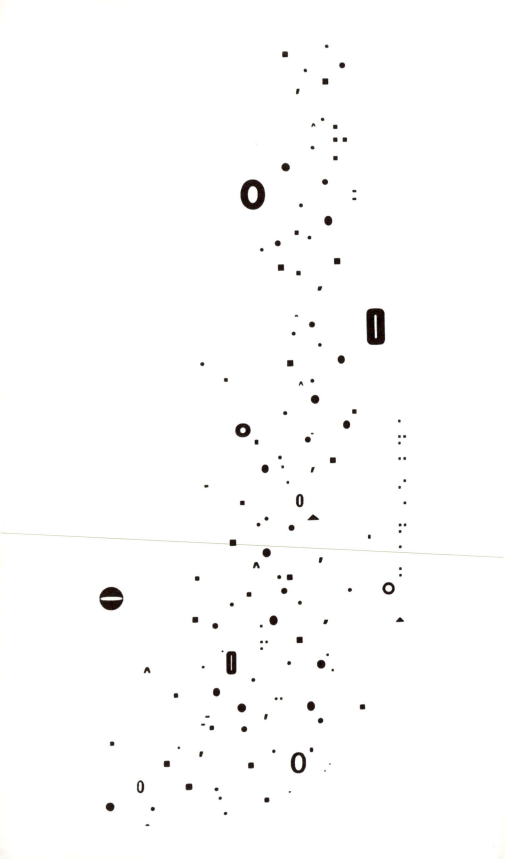

reangling the axes

against the vigilant
constellations
a cloud
of probabilities
(without
equations)

:

the pre
valence
of go
ing
on
rends
mourn
in
g

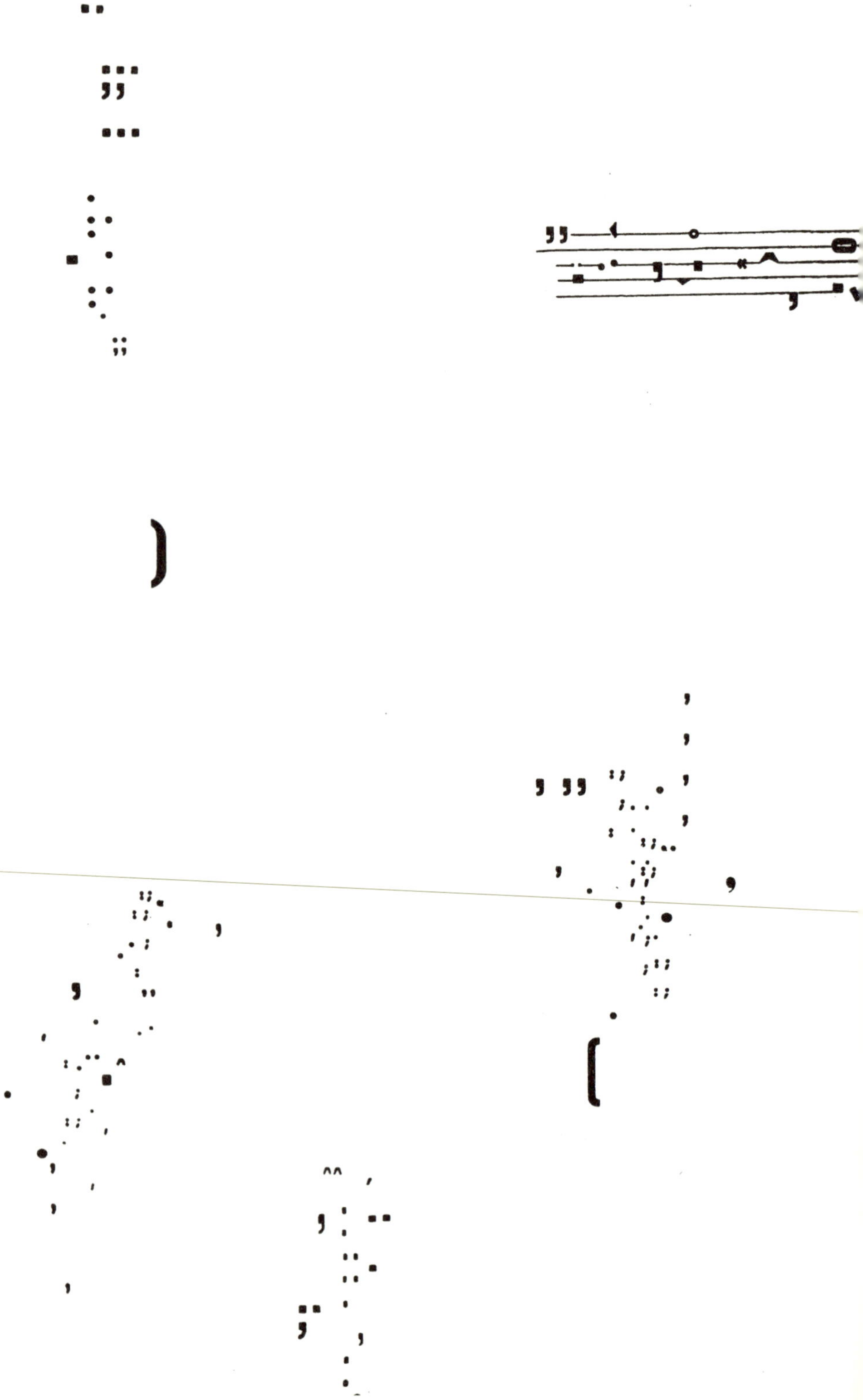

encounter

the crossing was
        arduous and
                dense with
                        creaking

                        in the words
                encountered
                        only frag
                                ments found

sea

                at
    the bottom of
            the abyss
                        the silent black
                current
                            the net of
                                    memories torn
                        :
            a tangle
    of north
            east
                south
                    west
                                no
                        more
                sextant

on/of

                              a bottle
                    thrown into the sea
              of the future
floats on
       the flow
                   of aimless
                          currents

        :   a form
       seeks
             the horizon
                   in the night

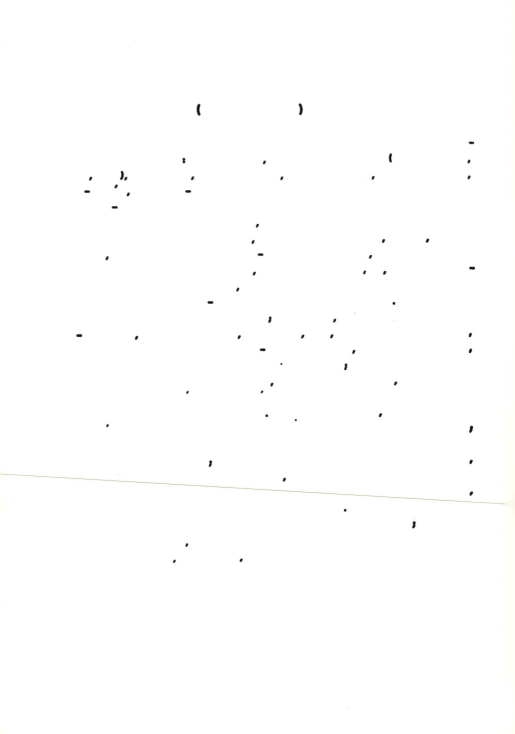

(a tangle)

                    in the
                    secret
                  nonbook
              of the
          mind
  a clutter
      (a tangle)
        of memories

                    friends
                        in flight
                            foolish flames   and

          sapphires
      despised
          by
              time

with the rest

          in
     Kepler'
s
atrium
     a banister in mourning
          and

               an ideogram was made with the rest

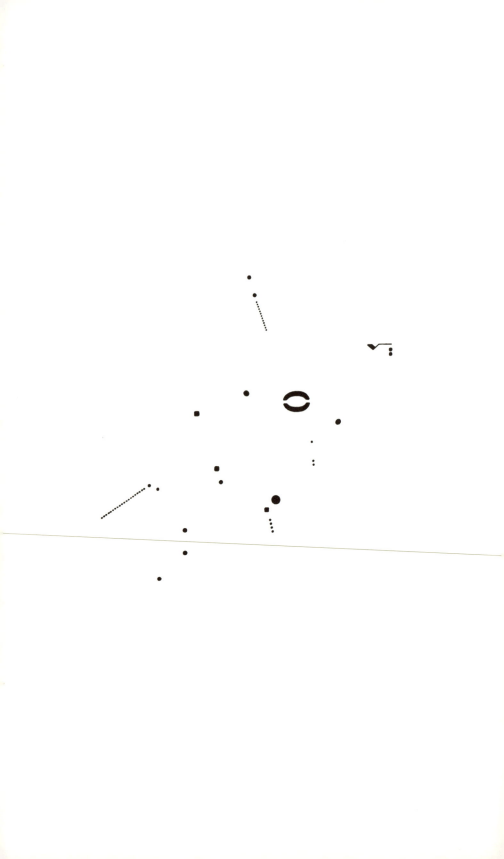

that

           the wadding of one
                         cloud
    fringes
             that
        the moon

      may shine
               a moment
as it passes
          frayed
                by the wind

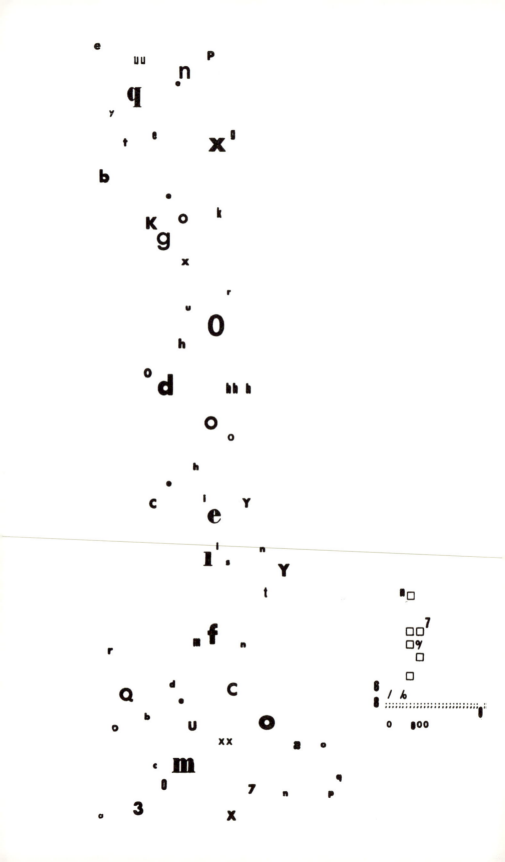

hieros gamos

we two going
   neither here   nor now
      (wherever   or never)

         without introduction   or matrix
      (without gestation

)

just like water flows through
a woolen thread from the fuller cup into the emptier
how fine it would be, o Glaucon,
if wisdom were made in such a way as to flow
through the letters of the alphabet
(drops the fragments)

— PLATO, *Symposium*

le
dieci porte
di
Zhuang-zi

the
ten Gates
of
Zhuang-zi

in memoriam Giacinto Scelsi

[1994]

TRANSLATION : *Giovanna Sandri*

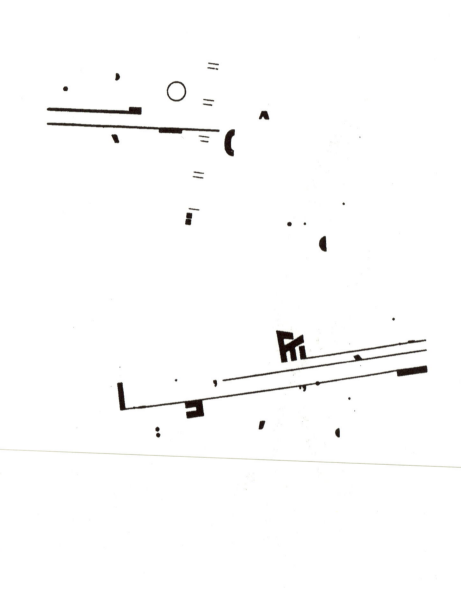

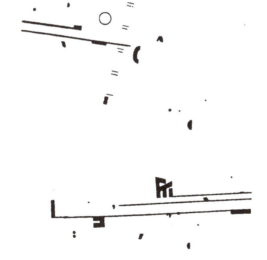

*la radice del suono (da **Zhuang-zi, XXII bis**)*

Intelligenza viaggiò verso nord
fino all'acqua oscura
e scalando il monte dell'Indistinto
al di sopra del tetto del mondo
entrò nelle vibrazioni del nonTempo
(ove la musica della Creazione
ha per strumenti le forze primordiali)

incontrò allora *Enunciato del non-agire*
e gli chiese:
vorrei farvi una domanda
per possedere il suono delle origini
da dove si parte
e quale strada si deve seguire?

Enunciato del non-agire non dette nessuna risposta
(non che non volesse
ma perché non sapeva che cosa rispondere   )

the soundroot (from Zhuang-zi, XXII B)

Intelligence *journeyed northward*
as far as the dark water
: climbing up the mountain of the Indistinct
above the roof of the world
he entered the vibrations of nonTime
(where the primordial forces
are the instruments of the music of Creation)

then he met Utterance of nonaction
and said to him:
I'd like to ask you a question.
To possess the sound of the origin
whence are we to start
and what road are we to follow?

Utterance of nonaction *gave no answer*
(he would but
he was unable to find an answer   )

il cielo e la terra sono di una bellezza maestosa
ma non ne parlano
le quattro stagioni si succedono secondo una legge evidente
ma non ne discutono
: a tutte le vibrazioni presiede un ordine costitutivo
ma esse non lo formulano

chi va alle sorgenti della radice del suono
(del cielo   della terra   del tuono   della notte   )
penetra l'ordine costitutivo di tutte le vibrazioni

qualcosa di estremamente terrificante e numinoso
si trasforma con le cento onde del suono

gli esseri di quaggiù
sono sottomessi fin dalle origini
alle vibrazioni di quelle onde
e ignorano la loro comune radice
perché è così che questi esseri esistono naturalmente
(dall'antichità ai nostri giorni   )

the sky and the earth are stately in their beauty
but they don't talk about it
the four seasons follow one another according to an evident law
but they don't discuss it
a constitutive order presides over all vibrations
but they don't formulate it

he who goes to the source of the soundroot
(of sky   earth   thunder   night   )
gets to the heart of the constitutive order
governing all vibrations

something extremely dreadful and numinous
changes with the one hundred soundwaves

since their origin, human beings
are subject to the vibrations of those waves
and yet they are unaware of that common root
for it is thus that these beings exist naturally
(from ancient times   to present times   )

lo spazio che si trova
tra i sei punti cardinali (benché immenso)
è vibrazioni ed accordi
la lanugine autunnale (benché minuscola)
è vibrazione e tensione

Vuoto e suono
Andromeda e filo d'erba
roccia e radice
seme ed acqua
minerale od ala
(tutti gli esseri) posseggono in sé vibrazioni e
(tuttavia) ne ignorano l'esistenza

(vibrazione è la radice dell'Universo)

colui che conosce questa radice comune
è degno di osservare il cielo
(i suoi occhi sono limpidi)
:
in lui armonie ed abissi
acque e tuono
sono
scale musicali
per ascendere
al

the space between the six cardinal points
(though immense)
is vibrations and chords
autumnal down (though tiny)
is vibration and tension

Void and sound
Andromeda and a blade of grass
rock and root
seed and water
mineral or wing
(all beings) possess in themselves vibrations and
(nevertheless) they are unaware of those driving forces

(vibration is the root of the universe)

he who knows this common root
is fit to observe the sky
(his eyes are limpid)
:
in him harmonies and abysses
water and thunder
are musical scales
for
ascending
to

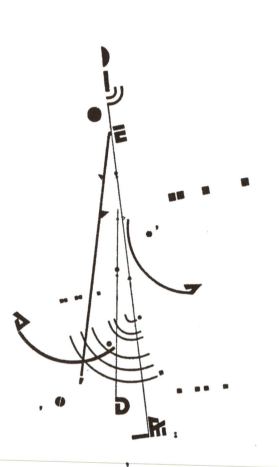

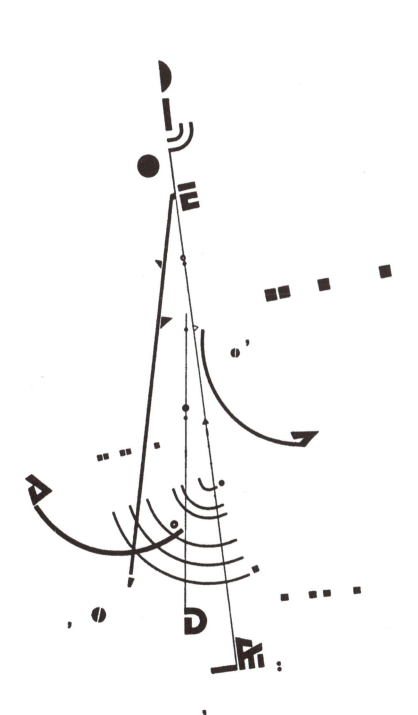

un giorno *Occhio-scintillante* incontrò
Radice-del-suono-errante e gli disse :

" fermati, ti prego   eri con me
sulle navi a Milazzo   e mio compagno,
seguace di Zhuang-zi

il vento Occidentale ha trasportato qui
dieci foglie marine   increspate dalle onde :
sono fogliesuono (suoni colorati)

i tuoi occhi sono limpidi
: tu puoi leggere ciò che vento ed acqua
hanno trascritto in quelle venature

le onde del suono ti guideranno   "

Occhio-scintillante scomparve e
le sue ultime parole si persero nel vento

Radice-del-suono-errante riuscì però ad afferrare
le dieci foglie marine   lievemente
dalle loro venature   ad uno ad uno
emersero   pensieri visibili

conosciuti (poi) come
le dieci porte di Zhuang-zi

:

one day Glittering-eye *came across*
Errant-root-of-sound *and said to him   :*

" *stop, please   you were with me*
in the ships at Mylae   and my companion,
follower of Zhuang-zi

the West Wind has carried here
ten sealeaves rippled by the waves   :
they are soundleaves   (coloured sounds)

your eyes are limpid
:   *you can read what wind and water*
transcribed in those veins

the soundwaves will guide you to   "

Glittering-eye *disappeared and*
his last words were lost in the wind

but Errant-root-of-sound *succeeded in*
grasping the ten sealeaves   lightly
one by one   visible thoughts
emerged from their veins

they are (later) known as
the ten Gates of Zhuang-zi

:

lentamente
(per gradi   )

Articolazione si avvicinò alla
prima Porta

scala discontinua di
lettere fu
Alfabeto

slowly

          (gradually   )

Articulation *approached*

    the first Gate

          a dis

          continuous staircase of letters

     was Alphabet

Benevolenza raggiunse

Ascolto alla

seconda Porta

insieme accolsero

Parola e

Verbo

Benevolence *joined*

Listening *at*

    the second Gate

        Both of them welcomed

    Word *and*

  Verb

Discorsività
                    trovò semichiusa

la terza Porta

                         troppi sentieri
              aveva seguito
                   per
                    Via

Discursiveness

found halfclosed

the third Gate

too many paths
he had followed
because of

Road

Quintessenza

sgusciò dalla
   quarta Porta

              : irrorò la campagna d'acqua
                    e   di   luce

Quintessence

stole away from

the fourth Gate

: the countryside was sprinkled
with water and   light

                                    alla quinta Porta
            Discordanza incontrò
                                    Differenza

    superata la soglia
                        trovarono
                                    Individualità

at the fifth Gate

Discordance *met with*

Difference

crossing the threshold

they found

Individuality

Abbandono

e *Grazia*

emersero dalla

sesta Porta

(tutta la valle   fu

illuminata

dal colore

Acceptance

        and Grace

loomed out of

    the sixth Gate

        (*the whole valley*

                was alight with

        color

superata la
settima Porta
apparve Sirio

formidabile
(impetuosa)
Ondulzaione ontologica
annullò ogni
tetto

beyond

        the seventh Gate

Sirius appeared

        formidable

(*impetuous*   )

      Ontological Undulation

               annulled   every

              roof

Connessione

si affacciò

dall'ottava Porta

con la potenza

dei sei soffi

esplorò

l'universo

Connection

                    leaned out

of the eighth Gate

            with the power
        of the six whiffs

                she explored

                    the
                        universe

attraverso
la nona Porta

(di   pietra   nera
di   pietra   bianca   )

Portatore-degli-Emblemi
incontrò *Abbandono-degli-Emblemi*

si scambiarono
uno jò-jò

ripresero direzioni
ellittiche

passing through
the ninth Gate

(*black stone*
     white stone   )

Emblem-Bearer
  came across Abandonment-of-Emblems

     they exchanged
   a yo-yo

          resumed elliptic
          directions

superata
la ringhiera delle parole

Zhuang-zi (infine   )
            si allontanò dalla
                        decima Porta

                                come goccia di pioggia
                        che quietolenta
            si stacchi da
                        foglia

leaving behind
the banister of words

Zhuang-zi (in the end   )
went away from
the tenth Gate

like a raindrop
quietslowly
dropping from
a leaf

Radice-del-suono-errante riprese il suo viaggio

                                              :

    fu fragore di rocce e di acque
silenzio di stelle

                    fu suono-sole-tuono
                    suono-spazio-sfera trasparente
                    pulsazione
                                        :

            è suono-spazio-tempo

    si dilata   sfuma in
            muta scia siderale nel
            curvo spazio di
            dilatata
        (dilatata   )
            sfera

    :

            è suoni-colori
    suoni-forme
                è esagoni armonici
                triangoli acuti
            ghiacci e
            foreste
            abissi e
            crepe
            e tonfi e
            precipizi

        (energia
            e creazione
)
            :
                da un suono-bolla
        vola una foglia-suono   cade una goccia
            cristallina lenta   ove (miniaturizzato)
            si può vedere   riflesso   l'universo
                    capovolto

                        ,

Errant-root-of-sound *resumed his journey*

                                       :

crash of rocks and water was he
silence of stars

                    sound-sun-thunder
                    sound-space-transparent sphere
                    vibration
                    :
          he is sound-space-time

      he widens out   fades away
          is a sidereal trail in the
          curve space   of an
          expanding
      (*expanding*)
          sphere

:

          he is sounds-colors
sounds-forms
          harmonic hexagons
          acute triangles
      glaciers and
      forests
      abysses and
      crevasses
      and thuds and
      precipices

    (*energy*
    and creation
)
    :
      from a sound-bubble
flies a leaf-sound a drop falls down
      a crystalclear lens in which (miniaturized)
      one can see reflected the universe
          overturned

            ,

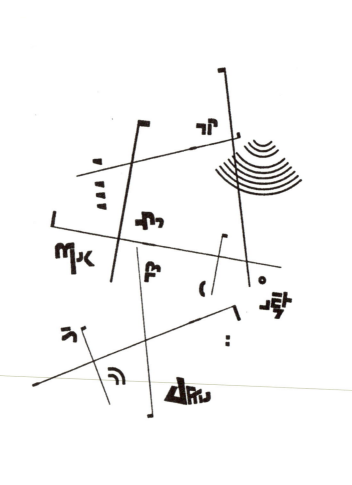

Così la neve al sol si disigilla,
Così al vento nelle foglie lievi
si perdea la sentenza di Sibilla

Dante, *Paradiso* XXXIII (64–66)

Even so the sunbeam doth the snow unseal
So was the Sibyl's saying lost inert
Upon the thin leaves for the wind to steal

Dante, Paradise XXXIII (64–66)

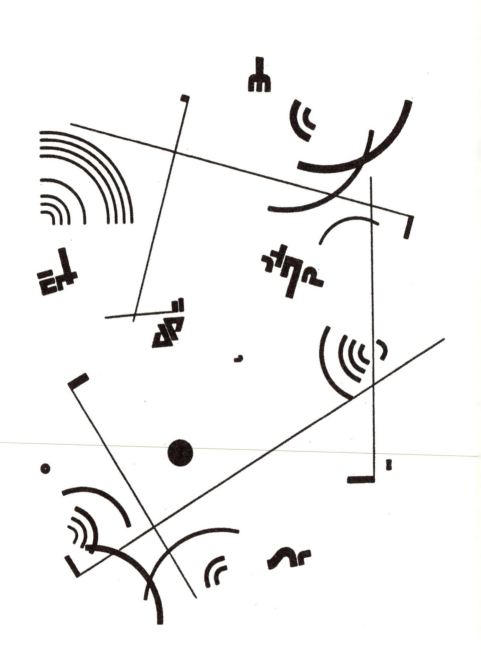

poesie
non
raccolte

uncollected
poems

(1987-98)

origine lunare dell'alfabeto

l'origine dell'alfabeto è strettamente legata
al concetto di tempo e di trasformazione

nella mitologia greca
Hermes è considerato l'inventore dell'alfabeto
in quella egizia è invece Thoth
(divinità corrispondente caratterizzata dal medesimo
concetto di trasformazione)

nella civiltà greca arcaica
questa origine è legata al ritmo delle stagioni (calendario)
in quella egizia
le letter sono inserite in una catena di eventi mistici
(: tutti gli dei sono lettere
            tutte le lettere sono idee
                    tutte le idee sono numeri
                            tutti i numeri   segni perfetti   )

Plinio riporta un'altra versione:
secondo Aristide l'invenzione dell'alfabeto è attribuita
a un sacerdote egizio di nome Meno (luna)
(anche Thoth era il dio della luna)

si legge in Plutarco
come gli antichi egizi chiamassero la loro terra Chemia
(*kemi* nella loro lingua significa *terra nera*)
da cui deriva alchemia (*al* è l'articolo in arabo)
originariamente la scienza ermetica sacerdotale
dell'antico Egitto

lunar origin of the alphabet

the origin of the alphabet is closely linked
to the concept of time and transformation

in Greek mythology
Hermes is considered the inventor of the alphabet
while in Egyptian mythology it is Thoth
(corresponding divinity characterized by the same
concept of transformation)

in Archaic Greece
its origin is linked to the rhythm of the seasons (calendar)
in Archaic Egypt
letters are included in a chain of mystic events
(: all gods are letters
    all letters are ideas
      all ideas are numbers
        all numbers   perfect signs   )

Pliny relates another version:
according to Aristides the invention of the alphabet is attributed
to an Egyptian priest named Meno (moon)
(Thoth was also the moon god)

then in Plutarch we read
that the ancient Egyptians called their land Chemia
(*kemi* in their language means *black earth*)
from which alchemy is derived (*al* being the article in Arabic)
originally the hermetic sacerdotal science
of ancient Egypt

dunque nella terra di Iside e del dio Sole (principio maschile)
che è anche la terra della trasformazione alchemica
toccò alla luna inventare l'alfabeto
la luna
che articola il mondo privo di luce della notte
(ombra sulle pietre
      rocce   alberi   foglie
         onde del mare   )

anche in Grecia troviamo la stessa origine lunare
: prima della introduzione dell'alfabeto fenicio modificato
esisteva infatti in Grecia un alfabeto segreto
custodito gelosamente dalle sacerdotesse della Luna (Io e le Parche)
era un alfabeto legato al calendario
le cui lettere non erano rappresentate da segni incisi
ma da ramoscelli recisi da alberi de specie diverse
che simboleggiavano i mesi dell'anno

le Parche dette anche Moire
(e *moira* in greco significa *fase*)
la luna ha infatti tre fasi e tre persone
:   la luna nuova   la dea vergine della primavera
        la luna piena   la dea ninfa dell'estate
           la luna calante   la dea vegliarda dell'autunno

il tempo del mese lunare
si apre al ritmo delle stagioni
e saranno ancora le Moire
che aiutano Hermes (la trasformazione) a comporre
l'alfabeto greco

therefore in the land of Isis and the Sun god (masculine principle)

which is also the land of alchemical transformation

it fell to the moon to invent the alphabet

the moon

which articulates the lightless world of the night

(shadow on stones

      rocks   trees   leaves

         waves on the sea   )

in Greece we find the same lunar origin

: before the introduction of the modified Phoenician alphabet

there was in fact a secret alphabet in Greece

jealously guarded by the priestesses of the Moon (Io and the Fates)

linked to the calendar it was an alphabet

whose letters were not represented by fixed signs

but by twigs cut from trees of various species

which symbolized the months of the year

the Parks also called Moirae

(and *moira* in Greek means *phase*)

the moon in fact has three phases and three persons

:   the new moon   the virgin goddess of spring

       the full moon   the nymph goddess of summer

          the waning moon   the venerable old goddess of autumn

the period of the lunar month

opens to the rhythm of the seasons

and again the Moriae

will help Hermes (transformation) to compose

the Greek alphabet

nel Vuoto di quella Notte
tra Dei che nascono
                    fuggono
                        intrecciano schemi
                            e comportamenti
si staccano
rami dagli alberi
(il Tempo si fa evento)

sono le Moire vestite di bianco le custodi segrete
dell'alfabeto arboreo
su quelle vesti lunari l'ombra dei primi segni alfabetici
filano tessono tagliano il tempo dell'uomo
scelgono recidono custodiscono l'alfabeto segreto
le stagioni / ritmo diventano il Tempo per l'uomo

a proposito della prima lettera dell'alphabeto greco, alfa,
Graves ricorda anche il fiume Alfeo (il più nobile dei fiumi)
così in questo divenire simbolico dello strumento
della comunicazione e della registrazione dell'accaduto (tempo)
il fluire dell'acqua è un altro elemento corrente
(perenne) (femminile)

anche nella lontana Irlanda
esisteva un alfabeto arboreo e sarà una versione nordica
dell'Ercole mediterraneo Ogma Volto di Sole
a sostituirlo con l'alfabeto Ogham
fornendo ai Bardi il loro bagaglio di conoscenze

dalle sacerdotesse della Luna
che custodivano l'alfabeto segreto legato ai cicli della terra
si passa alle fatiche d'Ercole
al lavoro dell'uomo (differenziazione)

in the Emptiness of that Night
among Gods being born
                    fleeing
                         weaving schemes
                              and behavior
branches
are snapped off trees
(Time is becoming an event)

clad in white the Moirae are the secret keepers
of the arboreal alphabet
on their lunar garments the shadow of the first alphabetical symbols
they spin weave cut the time of man
they select cut keep the secret alphabet
the seasons/rhythm become Time for man

regarding the first letter of the Greek alphabet, alpha,
Graves also mentions the river Alpheus (the noblest of rivers)
thus flowing water is another current element
(perpetual) (feminine)
in the symbolic coming into being of the instrument
for the communication and recording of the occurrence (time)

there was an arboreal alphabet
in far off Ireland as well and a nordic version
of the Mediterranean Hercules Sun-Faced Ogma will
replace it with the Ogham alphabet
providing the Bards with their store of knowledge

from the priestesses of the Moon
that kept the secret alphabet linked to the cycles of the earth
it is passed to the labors of Hercules
to the work of man (differentiation)

in un frammento di Nietzsche del 1898 si legge
   non si comunicano mai pensieri
si comunicano movimenti, segni mimici che vengono da noi letti
in chiave di pensieri

e quei segni mimici erano anche tracciati
dai ramoscelli recisi dalle sacerdotesse lunari
che intrecciavano con il Tempo la danza rituale dell'alfabeto

nei boschi di Psiche
(capillare) (incessante) è registrato quel ritmo / gesto
sacro alla sapienza (senza suono)
che si alfabetizza sulla strada della conoscenza

1978

Published in *Le Parole rampanti* 8/9 (1988)

in a fragment of Nietzsche from 1898 we read
    thoughts are never communicated
movements are communicated, mimetic signs which are read *by* us
as a key to thoughts

and these mimetic signs were also drawn
after twigs cut by the lunar priestesses
who with Time wove the ritual dance of the alphabet

in Psyche's woods
(vast) (never-ending) is recorded the rhythm / gesture
sacred to (soundless) wisdom
which is alphabetized on the road of knowledge

Translation: Guy Bennett

dall'Inno Omerico ad Hermes (frammenti)

sacro è il furto della trasformazione
divino fanciullo
ti cullavi con la tartaruga
Apollo si arrichì derubato
    spezzasti la prima canna rurale
              zufola la valle
    la porta chiusa aveva un foro
soffio di vento l'attraversa
          bibisgli il non detto
     giochi con la gioia
    jolly jolly jolly joker
araldo di vita   matto   cambia
      cambia con l'inganno

    frodi l'armento re degli animali
doni la lira a Apollo
           (Zeus se ne compiace)
       canti l'origine degli dei
     bardo della conoscenza
    sussurro alla sapienza
       maestro delle rune
messaggio dell'Ade
cambi il gioco del Re della Regina
        impronta di mago
nel capitombolo il tuo riso
gli dei indietreggiano
      rimani su una carta
funambolo bianco trapezio nero
    non spazio attraversato

from the Homeric Hymn to Hermes (fragments)

sacred is the transformation theft
divine child
ye were wont to be rocked by a turtle
on being robbed Apollo grew rich
      ye broke the primal rural reed
              piping is the valley
    the closed door had a hole
puff of wind flies through it
        ye whisper the unsaid
      play with the joy
     jolly jolly jolly joker
herald to life   madfool   change
     change by deceiving

    king of animals ye steal the herd by fraud
give Apollo a lyre
        (Zeus rejoices in it)
      singer of the Gods' origin
     bard of knowledge
      ye whisper to wisdom
        master of runes
Hades messenger
ye change the King's the Queen's play
      magician's print
in your thumbling your laughing
the Gods are to withdraw
     ye are left on a card
white rope-dancer black trapeze
    crossed nonspace

filo d'argento

la luna ha tante fasi

le inventi e non le sommi

luna bianca

luna nera   a

falce

eclisse

cambi nel gioco il gioco degli umani

nel solitario oracolare buffone

e guida

gli uomini non sanno

il Re è la Regina

la   Ruota il Carro   la Morte

la Giustizia

Temperanza la Forza

Torre la Stella

mercante inganna

inganna gli uomini

(maestri dell'inganno)

giura

giura

mentendo   il mondo non è

(sacro)

1978

Published as *Hermes the Jolly Joker* (1983)

          silver thread
        the moon has many phases
      ye invent them never sum them up
                              white moon
black moon
                    crescent
                          eclipse
on playing ye change the human being's play
in your solitary oracularity ye fool
                      and guide
                men are unaware
the King is the Queen
the   wheel the cart   Death
                            Justice
Temperance Strength
                      Tower the star
merchant   do deceive
                deceive all men
                    (masters of deceiving)
swear
do swear
lying   the world is not
                          (sacred)

Translation: Giovanna Sandri

da "in primavera ad Agra"

memoria (oltre

   : memoria dei nessi (dei collegamenti)
pretesa (inaudita) mai dove

dal
visibile / complesso
all'invisibile / semplice

impulso
che pervade
il timone primordiale
(totalmente
notturno)
oltre
il
cam
po

from "in spring at Agra"

memory (beyond

   : memory of connections (of links)
presumed (unheard of) never where

from the
visible / complex
to the invisible / simple

impulse
that permeates
the primordial helm
(entirely
nocturnal)
beyond
the
open
land

nel/nella

    e sarebbe pur bello
o Glaucone

se
   si potesse vedere
   il temporale procedere
   di una vis poetica

   sì che
   foglia fiore o frutto
   (inventato abisso
   capovolto)
   potessero sfogliarsi
   come
   un
   herbarium

   :

   nel
   giardino dei Semplici
   è la sorpresa
   che genera
   stupore

in/the

      and how fine it would be
  o Glaucon

if
   we could view
   the temporal passage
   of a vis poetica

   that
   leaf flower or fruit
   (fictitious abyss
   inverted)
   may be glanced through
   like
   an
   herbarium

:

     in the
     Garden of Simples
     lives the surprise
     that arouses
     wonder

(
    nella
    pianura
    di Aletheia
    la
    mobile radice

)

[senza titolo]

:

        dall'invisible
            centro
                del cerchio
                    il quadrato   from
                        del Dire   the invisible
                                            centre
                            of the circle
                            the square
                        of Saying

(
    in the
    level ground
    of Aletheia
    the
    moving root

)

[untitled]

:

    dall'invisible
        centro
            del cerchio
                il quadrato   from
                    del Dire   the invisible
                                        centre
                        of the circle
                        the square
                    of Saying

poiēsis)

(

orla
la
verità   it
                                                edges
periferia   truth
fatta presente
nel suo compiersi   a border
                                            made present
on its being fulfilled

il vasaio

nella
pietra del silenzio
come
in
uno   il
stampo   vasaio
                                        crea
il frutto
e questo lo chiamò
il dovuto

poiēsis)

(

orla
  la
    verità   it
                                         edges
    periferia   truth
     fatta presente
      nel suo compiersi   a border
                            made present
          on its being fulfilled

the potter

       in the
      stone of silence
   as
  in
a   the
  matrix   potter
              forms
        the fruit
     and this he called
      his due

la notte (del ricordo

      ritorna il grande Urano
portando
con sé la notte
          a Cipro
      cinta dal mare
il remo
(bianco)   del ricordo

epopteia

    viaggia
      sulla barca
della luna nuova
     l'obliquo
     dato
   visione
  danza
  contatto
 suono percepito
(non ancora ascoltato)

     in primavera
    ad Agra

the night (of memory

      the great Uranus returns
bearing
with it the night
              in Cyprus
          ringed by the sea
the (white)
oar   of memory

epopteia

    travelling
       on the boat
of the new moon
       the oblique
          fact
    vision
   dance
  contact
  perceived sound
(as yet unheard)

      in spring
       at Agra

enthousiasmos

le
Muse
anziane

figlie di
Urano

le
Muse
giovani

figlie di
Giove

(ti)
lasceranno
bere
e

la
bellezza era
sinapsi e vino

enthousiasmos

the
aged
Muses

daughters of
Uranus

the
young
Muses

daughters of
Jupiter

will let
(you)
drink
and

beauty
was
synapse and wine

e dono di Prometeo

il pitagorico Archita
avrebbe detto
:

il
numero
(

misura
armonia
)
è
pausa
(inter
vallo
)
tra
desiderio
e
Vuoto

(

tra
limitata
retta
e dilatato
specchio circolare

and gift of Prometheus

the Pythagoric Archytas
would have said
:

the
number

(

measure
harmony

)

is
a pause
(inter
val

)

between
desire
and
Void

(

between
limited
line
and dilated
circular mirror

canto di Arianna

gru

che tocchi l'argilla
e ti fai ombra
di un cuneo
sulla terra agra

volo cavo
di geometrie in bilico
sul labirinto
che avvolge e conferma

con
competenza sacra
nel tracciare
intrecciavi
sapienza e segno

che muta
filai in senso

Arianna's song

crane

on touching the clay
you become shadow
of a wedge-shaped sign
on the harsh ground

hollow flight
of geometries hovering
over the labyrinth
that enfolds and confirms

with
sacred skill
in tracing
you entwined
wisdom and sign

that silent
I spun into meaning

Ippolito scrive
che il Caldeo Zarata
disse a
Pitagora

:

dalla
reciproca indifferenza
un
incalcolabile
numero
di passi
(successivi)
in fuga
sempre più avvicinandosi
al divino
gioco del fanciullo
che
(occulto)
regge il mondo

Hippolytus writes
that Zaratas the Chaldean
said to
Pythagoras

                    :

                    from
                mutual indifference
            an
        incalculable
      number
  of (successive)
    steps
                        in flight
                    drawing ever nearer
                        to the divine
                            play of the boy
                        who
                        (concealed)
                            carried the world

in questa notte
del tempo del mondo

dai
dadi
di duro avorio
scompaiono
le tracce degli Dei

Orfeo non canta
sulla riva spenta
galleggia
la sua noce
senza coffa

discesa

abbandonati
i labirinti
· (tavole
degli Eventi

l'inutile sorpresa
(meta delusa)

:

nel grembo delle tenebre
la testa mozza d'Orfeo
attraversa
il linguaggio

(breve striscia di poi

in this night
of world time

from
the hard ivory
die
all traces of the Gods
disappear

Orpheus does not sing
on the dead shore
his shell
floats
without a maintop

descent

the labyrinths
abandoned
(tables
of Events

the useless surprise
(purpose betrayed)

:

in the womb of the darkness
Orpheus' mutilated head
traverses
language

(brief strip and then

gli uomini, lo stampo

Ea
Signore

gli
uomini
si lamentano

:
coloro
che
non sono
stati colpiti
dalla desolazione
(non si alzò più la calma quella notte)
costruirono uno stampo di mattoni

men, matrix

Ea
Lord

men
lament

:

those
who
have not
been struck
by grief
(rose no more the calm that night)
built a matrix of bricks

il ritorno

a Luigi Ballerini

funambolo in bilico
tra l'attrazione
della
Dimora e
la pulsione ad
errare
ritorna Ulisse

con
brocche d'acqua
(senza sale)
lava le orme del rischio
ove
l'inganno
scolma
la memoria

:

all'ombra
del remo (capovolto)
le
piaghe
del
soggiorno

Published in *Le Parole rampanti* 8/9 (1988)

the return

for Luigi Ballerini

tightrope walker poised
between the attraction
of
Home and
the urge to
wander
Ulysses returns

with
jugs of water
(saltless)
he washes away the traces of risk
wherein
deceit
empties
memory

:
in the shadow
of the oar (overturned)
the
sorrows
of the
stay

Translation: Guy Bennett

di/tra/di

peregrino di mari
tra scogli e scaglie
(partenze e ritorno)
Ulisse Ulisse
Ithaca ti fu vela
che non molla

noi
smarrita ogni Ithaca interiore
tra granchi di parole
anonimi andiamo
scafi
senza coffa
in attesa di un
gabbiano

to/in/for

        seafarer
    between cliffs and scales
            (departures and return)
Ulysses Ulysses
    to you Ithaca was a sail
        that does not unfurl

       every inner Ithaca lost
    in crabs of words
      anonymous we go
                hulls
            without a maintop
              waiting for a
                gull

sponda e soma :

gennaio argento
(novizio artiglio)
:

dal mare oscuro
anfora sottratta
la parola

pietra pesce
(furore e timbro)
sponda e soma
:

è la parola
che illumina
le stelle

enigma dello spazio

pende
sull'abisso
la parola fluente

colui che è senza
incalza l'oscura unione

nel progredire dell'evento
incatenare
enigmi e soluzioni

(sì che lo spazio
possa disprodursi

)

shore and vessel :

silver January
(novice claw)
:

from the dark sea
salvaged amphora
the word

stone fish
(fury and timbre)
shore and vessel
:

it is the word
that lights up
the stars

enigma of space

suspended
over the abyss
the flowing word

he who lacks
pursues the dark union

in the progress of the event
enigmas and solutions
must be bound

(that space
may disoccur

)

la scrittura
il Verbo

dallo sguardo dell'Evento
un velo bianco
nell'umidità
(ora lieve

ora pesante
)
della
scrittura

nella clessidra
(luogo del silenzio)
il Verbo sospeso
nel Vuoto

in alto all'alba

forti raffiche di vento
da nord-ovest   agitavano
le fronde degli alberi
quella mattina all'
alba
)

,
in alto
(a sinistra)
unica   una stella
firma il
cielo

writing
the Verb

gazing at the Event
a white veil
in the moistness
(now light
now heavy
)
of
writing

in the hourglass
(silent space)
the Verb hanging
in the Void

above at dawn

strong gusts of wind
from the northwest   shook
the branches of the trees
that morning at
dawn
)

,
above
(at left)
one   single star
signs the
sky

onde germoglia

nel luogo del desiderio   alle fibre dell'immediato
il bagliore neutro   l'oscillazione del
del Vuoto   riflesso

The preceeding six poems were previously unpublished. Sandri sent them to me in 1998 for inclusion in an issue of Paul Vangelisti's *Ribot*. They seem to be contemporary with the poems in *da "in primavera ad Agra"* which preceed them; indeed, two of the latter ("canto di Arianna" and "in questa notte del tempo del mondo") were included with these. For this reason they appear here without a separate series title. – GB

whence it sprouts

in the open space of desire   at the roots of the immediate
the neutral flash   the fluctuation of
of the Void   reflex

Translation: Guy Bennett

noi compagni di Ulisse
        (Argonauti dispersi

            per amore del sole che vi è caro
        (che ci fu caro)
delle gocce di pioggia
        di cui l'eco a volte percepiamo
                del placido chiarore lunare
                        sull'asfalto del mare
            dei cristalli di neve
        tra le ombre delle rocce
                di un febbraio che vi fu chiaro
                    (di una rosa   una pesca
                        di un tetto   di
                                un passo nella
                                        notte
)
            per amore del vento che
                    nelle lontane onde noi avvertiamo
        di una farfalla bianca   o
                    macolata
                        di quella stella dell'Arco che
                        voi   e noi   chiamammo Sirio
                    di un oleandro
                    (profumo dolceamaro)
                        (di una sosta
                                una svolta   di
                                    un risveglio
                                un richiamo
)

we companions of Ulysses
      (dispersed Argonauts

              for love of the sun that was dear to you
          (that was dear to us)
of the rain drops
          we sometimes hear in echo
                  of the calm lunar gleam
                          on the asphalt of the sea
              of the snow crystals
  in the shadows of the rocks
                  of a February that was clear to you
                      (of a rose   a peach
                          of a roof   of
                                  a step in the
                                      night
)

              for love of the wind that
                          in distant waves we warn
          of a butterfly white   or
                      maculate
                          of that star of the Bow that
                          you   and we   call Sirius
                  of an oleander
                      (bittersweet smell)
                          (of a pause
                              a turn   of
                                  an awakening
                                  a signal
)

per amore di quell'

indefinibile colore

di un albero in controlucerosa della

sera

(di un cancello socchiuso / semichiuso

di un merlo

un rosignolo

di uno

stupore

)

lasciate che

la morbida carezza del fianco

di un delfino bianco

ci protegga

che i flussiflutti

del mare le contorte lamiere della

nostra dimora

trasformino in

giardini

per ciò che a voi è sacro

(o profano)

noi   che fummo privati della vita

(quasi tutti noi giovani eravamo)

non private del

solo silenzio   che

oscuro ci

rimane

,

for love of that
indefinable color
of a tree   backlitpink in the
evening
(of a gate half-closed / ajar
of a blackbird
a nightingale
of an
astonishment
)

let
the soft caress of the flank
of a white dolphin
protect us
the waveflux
of the sea transform the twisted
sidings
of our dwelling into
gardens
for that which you hold sacred
(or profane)
we   who were deprived of life
(all of us nearly were young)
not deprived of the
only silence   that
sombre lingers
here

,

Ulisse
Ulisse
anche tu incontrasti
il ragazzo
la cui
barca
non
si
chiamava
ritorno

Published by Archivio di Nuova Scrittura (1998)

Ulysses
Ulysses
even you encountered
the boy
whose
boat
was
not
called
return

Translation: Guy Bennett

About the Author

Giovanna Sandri was born in Rome in 1923. She earned a degree in English literature from the University of Naples, writing her thesis on Ruskin's theory of aesthetics, and later taught English literature in Rome.

In the 1960s Sandri began creating works of visual poetry, which were included in exhibitions throughout Italy, as well as in Brazil, France, Holland, Israel, Japan, Sweden, the United States, and Uruguay. Her visual texts were also featured in the Quadriennale (1968), the Biennale di Bolzano (1969), the Biennale di Venezia (1978), and the Biennale di San Paolo (1981), and she had two solo exhibitions: "alfabeto/albero del Tempo," Galleria Civica d'Arte Modena, Palazzo Te, Mantua (1977), and "erörtern (occhi/tarocchi per estrarre segni)," Libreria Internazionale OOLP, Turin (1978).

Sandri contributed poems and essays to a number of magazines, including *Altri Termini, Anterem, Il Caffè, Il Cavallo di Troia, Chelsea, Green River Review, Grammatica, Harck, How(ever), Marcatrè, Periodo ipotetico, Programma, Ribot, Shantih, Shuttle, Tam Tam,* and *Uomini e idee.* In 1988 a special double-issue of *Le parole rampanti* was devoted to her work, which was also anthologized in *Antologija konkretne in vizualne poezije* (1978), *Italian Poetry Today* (1979), *Italian Poetry, 1960–1980: from Neo to Post Avant-garde* (1982), and *The Promised Land: Italian Poetry After 1975* (1997).

Sandri published five books of poetry – *Capitolo Zero* (1969), *da K a S (dimora dell'asimmetrico)* (1976), *Hermes the Jolly Joker* (1983; second edition, 1994), *clessidra: il ritmo delle tracce* (1992), recipient of the Premio Lorenzo Montano, and *le dieci porte di Zhuang-Zi / the ten Gates of Zhuang-zi* (1994) – and one poetic essay – *dal canguro all'aithyia (o come farsi scrittura)* (1981). In 1998, *hourglass: the rhythm of traces* (an English translation of her *clessidra*) was published by Mindmade Books. She also co-authored *il numero dimenticato – delle memorie ortogonali (o come il re si smarrì nel diafano)* (1988) with Madgalo Mussio.

Sandri died in Rome in 2002.

Bibliography

Capitolo Zero. Rome: Lerici Editore, 1969.

da K a S (dimora dell'asimmetrico) | *from K to S (ark of the asymmetric).* Translated by Faust Pauluzzi. New York, Norristown, Milan: Out of London Press, 1976.

> [*In the present edition we have changed the title of the translation from* ark of the asymmetric *to* dwelling of the asymmetric. *This rendering is both more literal and reflects Sandri's interest in Heidegger's writings on language and his belief that language is the dwelling ("dimora") of man.* – GB]

alfabeto/albero del Tempo. Mantua: Galleria civica d'arte moderna, Palazzo Te, 1977.

dal canguro all'aithyia (o come farsi scrittura). Rome and Venice: le parole gelate, 1981.

Hermes the Jolly Joker. Rome and Venice: le parole gelate, 1983; second edition, 1994.

Giovanna Sandri. Spec. issue of *Le Parole rampanti* 8/9 (1988).

clessidra: il ritmo delle tracce. Verona: Anterem Edizioni, 1992.

hourglass: the rhythm of traces. Translated by Guy Bennett. Los Angeles: Seeing Eye Books, 1998.

le dieci porte de Zhuang-zi | *the ten Gates of Zhuang-zi.* Translated by Giovanna Sandri. Rome: le parole gelate, 1994.

noi campagni di Ulisse (Argonauti dispersi. Milan: Archivio di Nuova Scrittura, 1998.

Acknowledgments

I would like to thank Paul Vangelisti for introducing me to the poetry of Giovanna Sandri. Had he not proposed that I translate one of her poems for his journal *Ribot* nearly twenty years ago, I might never have encountered her work, nor have had the pleasure of writing these words.

I also owe a special debt of gratitude to Luigi Ballerini. A close friend of Giovanna's, Luigi regularly brought me back books and notes from her on his return trips from Italy, and would occasionally regale me with anecdotes drawn from their friendship of many years. My knowledge of her work and what sense I have of her as a person would be considerably diminished were it not for his generosity.

My thanks also go to Dott.ssa Alessandra Mariani of the Biblioteca Nazionale Centrale di Roma for providing me with a scan of the special issue of *Le Parole rampanti* devoted to Sandri's work. I am very grateful to her for it, as I had unsuccessfully sought this issue for many years.

I am also grateful to Giulia Niccolai for her introduction, to Faust Pauluzzi for graciously permitting us to include his translations in this book, and to Flavio Ermini of Anterem Edizioni for permission to include excerpts of *clessidra: il ritmo delle tracce*.

Finally, I would like to thank Leonardo Campaner for his assistance in the preparation of this book. His careful reading of both the Italian texts and the translations, and his many insightful suggestions, have made this a better volume.

—Guy Bennett
October 2013

Other Titles from Otis Books | Seismicity Editions

Erik Anderson, *The Poetics of Trespass*
    Published 2010 | 112 Pages | $12.95
    ISBN-13: 978-0-979-6177-7-5
    ISBN-10: 0-979-6166-7-4

J. Reuben Appelman, *Make Loneliness*
    Published 2008 | 84 pages | $12.95
    ISBN-13: 978-0-9796177-0-6
    ISBN-10: 0-9796177-0-7

Bruce Bégout, *Common Place. The American Motel.*
Translated from the French by Colin Keaveney
    Published 2010 | 143 Pages | $12.95
    ISBN-13: 978-0-979-6177-8-2
    ISBN-10: 0-979-6177-8-

Guy Bennett, *Self-Evident Poems*
    Published 2011 | 96 pages | $12.95
    ISBN-13: 978-0-9845289-0-5
    ISBN-10: 0-9845289-0-3

Guy Bennett and Béatrice Mousli, Editors, *Seeing Los Angeles:*
A Different Look at a Different City
    Published 2007 | 202 pages | $12.95
    ISBN-13: 978-0-9755924-9-6
    ISBN-10: 0-9755924-9-1

Robert Crosson, *Signs/ & Signals: The Daybooks of Robert Crosson*
    Published 2008 | 245 Pages | $14.95
    ISBN: 978-0-9796177-3-7

Robert Crosson, *Daybook (1983–86)*
    Published 2011 | 96 Pages | $12.95
    ISBN-13: 978-0-9845289-1-2
    ISBN- 0-9845289-1-1

Mohammed Dib, *Tlemcen or Places of Writing*
Translated from the French by Guy Bennett
    Published 2012 | 120 pages | $12.95
    ISBN-13: 978-0-9845289-7-4
    ISBN-10: 0-9845289-7-0

Ray DiPalma, *The Ancient Use of Stone:*
Journals and Daybooks, 1998–2008
Published 2009 | 216 pages | $14.95
ISBN: 978-0-9796177-5-1

Jean-Michel Espitallier, *Espitallier's Theorem*
Translated from the French by Guy Bennett
Published 2003 | 137 pages | $12.95
ISBN: 0-9755924-2-4

Leland Hickman, *Tiresias: The Collected Poems of Leland Hickman*
Published 2009 | 205 Pages | $14.95
ISBN: 978-0-9822645-1-5

Norman M. Klein, *Freud in Coney Island and Other Tales*
Published 2006 | 104 pages | $12.95
ISBN: 0-9755924-6-7

Luxorius, *Opera Omnia or, a Duet for Sitar and Trombone*
Translated from the Latin by Art Beck
Published 2012 | 216 pages | $12.95
ISBN-13: 978-0-9845289-6-7
ISBN-10: 0-9845289-5-4

Ken McCullough, *Left Hand*
Published 2004 | 191 pages | $12.95
ISBN: 0-9755924-1-6

Béatrice Mousli, Editor, *Review of Two Worlds:*
French and American Poetry in Translation
Published 2005 | 148 pages | $12.95
ISBN: 0-9755924-3-2

Laura Mullen, *Enduring Freedom*
Published 2012 | 80 Pages | $12.95
ISBN-13: 978-0-9845289-8-1
ISBN-10: 0-9845289-8-9

Ryan Murphy, *Down with the Ship*
Published 2006 | 66 pages | $12.95
ISBN: 0-9755924-5-9

Aldo Palazzeschi, *The Arsonist*
Translated from the Italian by Nicholas Benson
  Published 2013 | 232 pages | $12.95
  ISBN-13: 978-0-9845289-9-8
  ISBN: 0-9845289-9-7

Dennis Phillips, *Navigation: Selected Poems, 1985–2010*
  Published 2011 | 288 pages | $14.95
  ISBN-13: 978-0-9845289-4-3
  ISBN-10: 0-9845289-4-6

Antonio Porta, *Piercing the Page: Selected Poems 1958–1989*
Translated from the Italian by Anthony Baldry, Rosemary Leidl, et al
  Published 2011 | 368 pages | $14.95
  ISBN-13: 978-0-9845289-5-0
  ISBN-10: 0-9845289-5-4

Eric Priestley, *For Keeps*
  Published 2009 | 264 pages | $12.95
  ISBN: 978-0-979-6177-4-4

Ari Samsky, *The Capricious Critic*
  Published 2010 | 240 pages | $12.95
  ISBN-13: 978-0-979-177-6-8
  ISBN-10: 0-979-6177-6-6

Hélène Sanguinetti, *Hence This Cradle*
Translated from the French by Ann Cefola
  Published 2007 | 160 pages | $12.95
  ISBN: 970-0-9755924-7-2

Janet Sarbanes, *Army of One*
  Published 2008 | 173 pages | $12.95
  ISBN-13: 978-0-9796177-1-3
  ISBN-10: 0-9796177-1-5

Severo Sarduy, *Beach Birds*
Translated from the Spanish by Suzanne Jill Levine and Carol Maier
  Published 2007 | 182 pages | $12.95
  ISBN: 978-9755924-8-9

Adriano Spatola, *The Porthole*
Translated from the Italian by Beppe Cavatorta and Polly Geller
    Published 2011 | 112 pages | $12.95
    ISBN-13: 978-0-9796177-9-9
    ISBN-10: 0-9796177-9-0

Adriano Spatola, *Toward Total Poetry*
Translated from the Italian by Brendan W. Hennessey and Guy Bennett,
with an Introduction by Guy Bennett
    Published 2008 | 176 pages | $12.95
    ISBN-13: 978-0-9796177-2-0
    ISBN-10: 0-9796177-3-1

Carol Treadwell, *Spots and Trouble Spots*
    Published 2004 | 176 pages | $12.95
    ISBN: 0-9755924-0-8

Allyssa Wolf, *Vaudeville*
    Published 2006 | 82 pages | $12.95
    ISBN: 0-9755924-4-0